Praise for
Infinite Life, Infinite Lessons

"Susan Grau is the real deal! Her words are a guide to tapping into our own intuition and staying in communion with loved ones on the other side. Her messages reveal the truth of the love that all of us are made of."
— **Dr. Laura Berman,** best-selling author, therapist, grieving mama, and host of *Language of Love*

"Infinite Life, Infinite Lessons *is a captivating narrative of a near-death experience and a profound journey of personal growth through adversity. This story emphasizes that life's toughest trials can reveal profound self-discoveries and a renewed sense of purpose, illuminating the meaning of the afterlife and our unbreakable connection with universal spiritual energy. A must-read."*
— **Anita Moorjani,** *New York Times* best-selling author of *Dying to Be Me* and *Sensitive Is the New Strong*

"It's hard not to wonder how our lives might be different if we could learn how to reach our soul's highest potential. Infinite Life, Infinite Lessons *is an extraordinary journey into the spirit-affirming world of intuition, awareness, and life beyond the limited constructs of our mind. Susan's story of spiritual discovery is both courageous and heart healing. She inspires us to overcome our fear of truly being known and lays a path so we, too, can awaken to the magnificence of our own soul's seeing. This is a call to become bold and fearless, to walk our very own Yellow Brick Road, and discover the soul path of embodied love."*
— **Dr. Michele Kambolis,** author of *When Women Rise: Everyday Practices to Strengthen Your Mind, Body, and Soul*

Infinite Life, Infinite Lessons

Hay House Titles of Related Interest

All of the above are available at your local bookstore,
or may be ordered by visiting:

Hay House USA: www.hayhouse.com®
Hay House Australia: www.hayhouse.com.au
Hay House UK: www.hayhouse.co.uk
Hay House India: www.hayhouse.co.in

Infinite Life, Infinite Lessons

Wisdom from the Spirit World on
Living, Dying, and the In-Between

SUSAN GRAU

HAY HOUSE LLC
Carlsbad, California • New York City
London • Sydney • New Delhi

Published in the United States by: Hay House LLC: www.hayhouse
.com® • *Published in Australia by:* Hay House Australia Publishing Pty
Ltd: www.hayhouse.com.au • *Published in the United Kingdom by:*
Hay House UK Ltd: www.hayhouse.co.uk • *Published in India by:* Hay
House Publishers (India) Pvt Ltd: www.hayhouse.co.in

Cover design: Shubani Sarker
Interior and jacket design: Julie Davison
Author photo: Justin Chee

**Cataloging-in-Publication Data
is on file with the Library of Congress**

Hardcover ISBN: 978-1-4019-7723-8
E-book ISBN: 978-1-4019-7724-5
Audiobook ISBN: 978-1-4019-7725-2

10 9 8 7 6 5 4 3 2 1
1st edition, July 2024
Printed in the United States of America

This product uses responsibly sourced papers and/or recycled materials.
For more information, see www.hayhouse.com.

SUSTAINABLE
FORESTRY
INITIATIVE

Certified Chain of Custody
Promoting Sustainable Forestry
www.forests.org
SFI-01268

SFI label applies to the text stock

This book is dedicated to the most important people in my life: my family. Your love and encouragement have been the driving force behind every word on these pages. Thank you for always believing in me and for being my constant source of strength. I love you all!

CONTENTS

Foreword

Life is an enigmatic tapestry of joy and sorrow, love and loss, triumphs and tribulations. In *Infinite Life, Infinite Lessons*, Susan Grau shares her profound and awe-inspiring story of struggle, loss, and her near-death experience, leading to a transformative journey that has the power to heal and inspire countless others.

Susan's tale is not just a chronicle of her life and lessons but a profound narrative of human resilience and the unyielding strength of the human spirit. From her earliest days of hardship to the arduous road of loss she faced, including the heart-wrenching suicide of her beloved family members, her story resonates deeply with our own struggles and aspirations. Her courage in opening her heart to vulnerability and sharing her innermost experiences allows readers to connect on a profound level and find solace in the understanding that they are not alone in their challenges.

Throughout *Infinite Life, Infinite Lessons*, Susan embarks on an extraordinary journey of self-discovery and spiritual awakening. Her near-death experience provided a gateway to an unseen realm, offering her glimpses of profound insights and wisdom that she brings back to this earthly plane. These invaluable lessons offer a lifeline to those navigating their own tumultuous paths, granting hope in times of despair and inspiring faith in the face of adversity.

As you delve into these pages, you will undoubtedly be moved by Susan's incredible resilience, her unwavering faith, and her willingness to embrace life's challenges as opportunities for growth. She skillfully weaves together her personal experiences with insights and teachings that extend far beyond her own story. With humility, grace, and authenticity, she illuminates the pathway to healing, showing us how our greatest challenges can become the catalysts for transformation and self-awareness.

Her profound understanding of the afterlife, gained through her near-death encounter and the countless readings she has given to the masses, will leave you with a newfound sense of hope and connectedness to something greater than ourselves. She invites us to explore the possibilities of life beyond the physical, offering comfort to those who have lost loved ones and sparking a renewed curiosity about the mysteries that lie beyond the veil.

This book is not just a memoir but also a self-help guide packed with empowering lessons and practical exercises aimed at aiding others on their unique journey of healing and self-discovery. Susan encourages us to delve into the depths of our emotions, embrace vulnerability, and nurture our souls on the path to healing and self-empowerment. Each lesson she imparts acts as a stepping stone, guiding us to face our grief, uncertainties, and challenges head-on as we make our way toward a place of greater self-awareness, forgiveness, and acceptance.

Susan's story is a powerful reminder that life's trials need not define us; instead, they serve as both purpose and reward toward greater wisdom and compassion. Her journey, filled with Integration Moments that illuminate the path toward healing, resonates deeply with those who seek to find meaning in their own struggles and come out stronger on the other side.

With an open heart and a receptive mind, let Susan Grau's *Infinite Life, Infinite Lessons* be a guiding light on your personal journey of healing and self-discovery. May her profound insights and spiritual awakening inspire you to embrace life's challenges, navigate through the darkest of days, and discover the infinite lessons that await you along the way.

If you follow and apply the practical knowledge Susan offers in this incredible masterpiece, you will make the rest of your life, the *best* of your life. *Infinite Life, Infinite Lessons* deserves a permanent place on your bookshelf, just as it has on mine!

— **Kim Russo**, The Happy Medium,
intuitive counselor, author, host of A&E's
Celebrity Ghost Stories and *The Haunting of . . .*
www.Kimthehappymedium.com

Introduction

The Journey Beyond

"How much of your story are you going to tell?" my agent asked me as I began the journey of writing the book you're now holding in your hands.

"Enough that others understand that my life is no different from theirs," I replied.

Why would people think my life is different from theirs? Well, because I talk to dead people! Communicating with the unseen world of spirit has been a part of me since birth. I had more "imaginary" friends than you could count—but, I've come to find out, they were as real as it gets. I learned this during a near-death experience that set the foundation of my life and serves as the starting point of this book.

While touring the afterlife with an angelic entourage, I was shown without a shadow of a doubt that life is infinite and that the point of our human experience is to evolve our souls through the choices we make and the lessons we learn from those choices. The world of spirit is beautiful, blissful, light, and endlessly loving—it's perfect. In other words, it is the opposite of *this* world. You don't need me to tell you how full of sorrow this planet can be; you can easily turn on your favorite news channel for that. However, what I *am* here to tell you is that the darkness of this world is what we *need* to experience to achieve our mission of soul growth.

Think about it like the stars backdropped by the black of space—if there were no outer-space dark, we wouldn't see their heavenly light, and we wouldn't even know they existed. Similarly, in the spirit world, it is *all* love and light; we come to earth, this world of duality, to learn how bright we truly are. It may be difficult to believe if you're prone to feeling the weight of this imperfect world deeply, but the truth is, our souls *want* to be here because they understand that we need the contrast to really *know* what we are made of.

If you are at the point in your own spiritual journey where you're ready to *know* what you are made of, this book is for you. *Infinite Life, Infinite Lessons* was designed for the soul who is ready for growth and change, the soul who craves to know if there is more to our existence than just this human experience, the soul who wants to learn about the afterlife and how it informs the meaning of our human lives, and, of course, the soul who wants to know where their loved ones have gone after leaving this planet. It is for the soul who is ready for true *spirit consciousness*, which is being conscious of the spirit realm that resides in us, through us, and all around us. Once we understand that, we realize we are never separated from the universal energy of Spirit.

I would say this book was a labor of love, but in all honesty, for me, it was a grueling trip down painful-memory lane. While writing *Infinite Life, Infinite Lessons*, I found that sharing my vulnerable, sometimes heart-wrenching journey was challenging because pain and suffering certainly have been at the forefront of my journey, and digging that up for the world to see isn't exactly *fun*. But I knew that sharing my intimate story was something I *must* do to help you understand that you are *not* alone in your struggles.

I am in no way immune to suffering merely because I've visited and communicated with the spirit world my entire life. And the truth is that no one is. Challenges, suffering, loss—it is simply a part of the human condition. And, as spirits showed me during my near-death experience, and as I attempt to explain throughout the course of this book, it's an essential part in prompting our soul-growth journey.

Like you, I have lived a life full of love and loss, pain and joy, trauma and healing. As an abuse survivor, empath, and intuitive medium, my heart has weathered many storms on an intimate level, including the rippling effects of losing my two brothers and mother to suicide, which has left an indelible imprint on my soul. I know your path has been laced with challenges that left their marks and deep wounds on your soul too. In writing this book, I hope to illuminate that it's through these seemingly negative experiences that we are granted an invitation to discover deep insights into the essence of who we truly are, why we are here, and where we are going.

Experiencing deep grief is often a catalyst to exploring life's biggest questions. Beginning with my near-death experience and continuing with the winding journey toward my life as a professional spiritual medium, this book is full of answers from the spirit world to those big questions. Many of you holding this book may also know grief intimately and may be looking for greater understanding and solace. My hope is that *Infinite Life, Infinite Lessons* will help you understand *why* we experience hardship, *where* your loved ones are in spirit, *what* the afterlife is like, and *how* to grow and expand in the wake of their death into the beautiful soul that Spirit created uniquely for *you*.

I use the word *Spirit*, capitalized, to represent a deity— *God, Source,* the *Universe,* or whatever word resonates with you. The word *spirit*, lowercase, represents our loved ones and souls on the other side, including the angels and spirit guides. The *afterlife, other side, spirit world,* and *world of spirit* all denote our home—the vibrational realm where we have come from and will return to.

We were created with the inherent strength to heal our wounds and transmute our pain into our power. At the end of this writing process, I see that the pain, once again, has served me. Coming into a place of deeper self-awareness, I've been able to reach into the dark cracks of myself and fill them with a shine of gold. And that is what I hope for you, too, dear reader.

You may feel a deep vulnerability arise in you while you progress through these pages, as I felt in writing it, and I want to prepare you for that. But the truth is, I *want* to crack you open—just enough to take the next steps in healing the broken pieces of your heart, just as I have healed mine.

I have learned to embrace my pain instead of running from it. I have accepted as truth what the angels shared with me when I was a child during my near-death experience: "What you run from chases you, and what you try to control controls you." Facing my truth and my shadow head-on has transformed me more than I could have ever imagined, and my primary purpose in writing this book was to offer you practical tools to help you better navigate your life journey—the same tools I have used to navigate mine. The end of each chapter contains Integration Moments and exercises designed to help you delve deeper into your soul so that you can heal and see the value of *you*! (You'll need a separate journal to write about the prompts contained in the Integration Moments as well as to do many of the chapter exercises.)

As you read *Infinite Life, Infinite Lessons*, please know that in writing it, I wanted you to know that someone was beside you as you sort through the dark mud of your life, someone who understood the hardships of walking the soul path and, ultimately, has learned how to endure and thrive *because of* pain, not *in spite of* it. I have always thought the term "in spite of" had a negative connotation and "because of" offered empowerment. So then: *because of* my strength to grow through adversity, I thrived. I worked hard to see the truth of my soul journey. If you are reading this, you, too, are ready to work hard to know your truth and set foot onto your soul path. My greatest hope is that by sharing *my* dark, it brings you even just a little bit closer to *your* light.

Welcome to the journey beyond!

Lovingly,
Susan

CHAPTER 1

The Light within the Darkness

"Your baby's in the freezer." These cautionary words boomed, unmistakably, in my mother's ear. She was no stranger to hearing odd voices—in fact, my father not too long before this had her hospitalized for just that—but this message seemed preposterous. Loud but preposterous. *Impossible*, she assured herself, *just my mind playing tricks on me.* She pushed the thought away and continued vacuuming the house as I, on the verge of death, screamed, "Mommy!" over and over again, trapped inside the garage freezer.

I wasn't at risk from the cold; the appliance was unplugged, tucked in a corner and forgotten. All I could sense was the dark. Stale dark. Musty dark. An old closet in an abandoned house full of century-old dust dark. As a four-and-a-half-year-old, I was accustomed to being afraid of the night. But this? This dark was different. In contrast to the imagination-fueled fears that small children often feel while tucked alone in their beds, this dark was haunting—and I knew I was in terrible danger.

I say I was four and a half, but really I was tipping on five if I want to be exact—and I do. Memories are built to blur over time, especially childhood memories that are difficult to summon. Still, I remember this day as precisely today as the day it happened. It turns out, a visit to the other side is impossible to forget.

The day began with joy. I'd been playing with two boys, who were a year older than I was, in my hometown in Southern California, and we had been picking blackberries and gulping them down like candy. We were having fun outside for quite a while when we decided to build a fort in the grove near my house.

"But first," one of the boys turned to me and announced, "if you want to keep playing with us, you have to get us Popsicles."

Of course, I did want to play fort—it was one of my favorite games—so I did as my seniors demanded, even though it meant breaking the rules. I was not allowed to go into the garage, where the Popsicle freezer was, without permission. But attention came slow in my home. I was a somewhat reserved child, so I remember feeling genuinely happy on this friend-filled day and would do anything to keep playing. As the boys yelled out the flavors they wanted me to grab for them, I headed toward the garage, excited for what promised to be a wonderful afternoon full of Popsicles, friends, and forts. As I climbed onto the ledge of the upright freezer and reached up on my tippy toes to retrieve our treats, I remember looking in and seeing only the back of the freezer. There was nothing in it at all besides the shelves. In fact, it didn't even have any lights on.

Oh, I thought to myself, *why isn't it working?*

As the thought was still settling in my mind, I began to turn and relay the sad news that there were, in fact, no Popsicles. But before the words could come out of my mouth and before my body could entirely turn around, I felt the freezer door slam shut hard on my backside, locking me in. I was stuck between the heavy door and the inside of the dank freezer—and in between life and death, I would soon come to learn.

Facing inward with my hands held above my head (I had still been reaching up high to where I thought the Popsicles were when I was shut in), I was unable to move my arms or turn around. I heard the boys' laughter on the other side of the door—it sounded far away but so close . . . as if I could nearly touch it and join in the fun. As if I, too, could be in on the joke. But soon, the laughter faded, followed by a loud thud. The boys had closed the garage door, sealing me to my fate. No one was joking. Then nothing. Silence.

My mind struggled to understand what was happening and why. Surely the boys didn't intend to leave me here like this . . . ? Why would that be fun for anyone? This must be a misunderstanding. But soon enough, the terror set in that I was, in fact, abandoned, and I heeded the call of survival the only way I knew how: I began to scream. And scream and scream and scream. But nobody came. As time slowly, excruciatingly crept forward, my cries intensified, becoming louder and primal—like a wild animal caught in a cage. And isn't that precisely what I was? The cage I found myself in was a 1950s freezer, so everything about it was too heavy for my tiny self to push or open or lift. I would spend what my mother later said was between 30 minutes to two hours trapped there; to me, it felt like minutes and an eternity all at once. We will never know for sure, but odds are the truth lies somewhere in the middle.

With my back smashed against the door and my front against the freezer's insides, my entire body was being squeezed, and it was becoming increasingly difficult to breathe. Is this what my aunt felt when she was lying in "the box," white and pale, stiff, when they, too, closed the lid? Was I in my own box like her? Was I going to die? Survival instinct has no age. From our first to our last breath, we know when we are in grave danger and intuitively do whatever we must to stay alive. Our souls are built for survival—it's part of our DNA. We have an innate sense that we must live out our agreed-upon soul's journey (but more on that later).

As I began to lose consciousness, the fear ramped up into full-blown panic, and my world started spinning. I squirmed frantically and tried everything to wiggle the freezer door open, but nothing would budge. I screamed for what felt like forever, fighting for survival with each shallow breath, stranded alone in the darkest dark I had ever experienced.

And then suddenly, the lights appeared.

"Stop screaming," a strange but warm voice said. "We're going to get your mommy."

I saw three distinct white lights in the freezer with me—one brilliant bright light in the foreground and two slightly dimmer lights on each side. On the verge of suffocation, I felt dizzy and confused, yet simultaneously increasingly calmer. I was disoriented, but somehow I knew it was the brightest light that was speaking to me.

"Stop screaming," the light said again softly. "We're going to get your mommy, but first there are some things we want to show you."

Still, I couldn't stop wailing. Despite how magnetic and comforting these lights felt, I was too terrified to do anything other than continue the frantic survival dance with what little energy I had left, giving my all to breaking free of the coffin tightening around me.

My mother was a busy 1960s housewife with four children, an alcoholic husband, and a million other daily things to manage; an unplugged freezer in a garage we hardly used was the least of her worries. Yet she heard it as clear as crystal that day: "Your baby's in the freezer." She ignored that first message, as we often do with our intuition, and continued her household chores. She pushed that dark thought out of her soul while mine went whirling into the light.

The First Cracks in the Vase

I think of a newborn baby like a rare, perfect vase. Everything about it is whole. Yet, given time, each and every whole and perfect child will chip, will crack, will shatter. For some, it will take a long time, and for others no time at all. My fate was to be in the latter group.

I was somewhere between three and four when I was first molested, a trauma that continued throughout much of my childhood and gradually escalated into being trafficked throughout my neighborhood. It began with some boys in the community who were about five years older than me. They would take me behind the house next door, which we called "the Addams Family house" because it had a big "A" on the chimney. These older boys would do unspeakable things to me, taking full advantage of my trust and innocence. Looking back, I realize that those boys, whether they were aware of it or not, were essentially grooming me for the adults, who were pornographers who trafficked many children in the neighborhood.

When most people hear the word *traffic*, they picture a child being stolen and sold with the help of some elaborate underground tunnels. While that certainly happens, the raw truth is that most trafficking occurs in the neighborhoods where the children live, with people they know and trust. Many aren't stolen at all, and that was the case for me—I was regularly abused right in my own neighborhood, unbeknownst to my parents.

That might be hard to comprehend, how my parents couldn't know. But it was a different time back then—long before "helicopter parenting"—when kids would be out of the house all day doing all kinds of crazy things without supervision. Additionally, my parents, being from small-town Iowa, were extremely naïve to this kind of evil, as they had never heard of anything so horrendous happening in their communities before. On top of all that, my mother was on a cocktail of pills for her "condition," rendering her largely absent in mind. All these factors allowed the abuse to continue for years in plain sight.

So, why didn't I tell my parents? Many people have asked me that. When the abuse started, I was so young that I didn't even really understand that something bad was happening to me. As I got older, it was made very clear by the perpetrators that "tattling" to my parents was not an option. Keep in mind this was not just happening to me but also to many children in the community—my friends, my siblings—so I genuinely thought that it was "normal." As heartbreaking as it is looking back, as heartbreaking as it is to say out loud now, *abuse was my normal.*

I'll never forget the day I learned it was actually not normal at all. My nana was in charge of us kids while our parents were out, and I was calling her from my abuser's house to update her on my whereabouts, as I intended to stay out later than we had agreed upon.

"Hi, Nana. Is it okay if I stay a bit longer and go swimming with my friends?" I asked her.

"Okay, darling, that's fine. Just come home and pick up your bathing suit. I will get it ready for you," she replied.

"It's okay," I said. "I don't need one, Nana."

"What do you mean you don't need one? Of course you need one . . ."

"No, I really don't—no one wears clothes here, ever, Nana!"

"What?!" she was nearly screaming in alarm. "Susie, come home immediately."

At that moment I *knew*. I finally understood that whatever was happening to me and around me was not normal at all. However, I instantly felt guilty because I thought it was *me* who had done something wrong.

Unfortunately, this was a secretive era; people rarely acknowledged or spoke about anything real like this. Because my nana thought it was a one-time event, she never sincerely discussed the abuse with me, my parents, or anyone else. Therefore, this way of life continued to be my reality until I was nine, at which point we moved to a new neighborhood. By then I knew what was happening to me was "bad," but I hoped our family's move out of that neighborhood would be my saving grace. Sadly, abuse was still lingering around the corner, waiting for me in my new city.

I now know that once you've been abused, you tend to become a target for more abuse. If you haven't healed and been protected, which I hadn't, abusers can sniff you out. It's like you have a target on your back; and that is what happened to me. Most of my childhood was tainted with this abuse, and it has been one of the great wounds of my life to heal.

The Light through the Cracks

Why do spiritually inspired creations have to grow up and experience pain? And seemingly perpetual pain at that. There are many beautiful things about this human experience, but without exception, we have all, at some point, looked at our broken pieces and asked ourselves, "Why me?" I know I did once I fully understood the horrible things that had happened to me as a child; and I'm sure you have, too, when it comes to your own unique challenges.

As the Buddha discovered, suffering is the human condition. My forays into the afterlife, including my own near-death experience, and subsequent decades working as a spiritual medium have further demonstrated this. Life is a journey of lessons—lessons to be learned through both joy and pain. Pain can be our greatest teacher, and lessons ultimately become our blessings if we can lean in to our challenges. We must pivot thoughts away from *Why me?* to *What is the lesson in this for me?* Then we will come into alignment with our soul's highest growth, our soul purpose, which is indeed the point. We understand that humans are meant to crack because our souls are meant to grow. We need those breaks to allow for the light to get in.

While writing this book, I debated how much of my childhood abuse my readers needed (or wanted) to hear. But in my heart, I know that the spirit world wants me to use my experience to explain how this trauma, this crack—in addition to all the other ones that have occurred since—helped strengthen my faith in Spirit and pave the way for me to help others. That is what I *chose* to do with my challenges. Our choices are everything, as you will learn in this book. Everyone has wounds, traumas, challenges, cracks—it's what we choose to do with them that matters.

The sexual abuse I endured was the initial blemish on my childhood perfection, but because of my young age, denial was easy and effective. The crack that followed, my near-death experience in the freezer, was impossible to ignore. This time, I knew I was suffering, I knew I was in grave danger, and I knew I might die. Despite being the most terrifying experience of my life, it too was one of the brightest moments, brimming with profound lessons I would carry with me forever. The truths I learned then about the afterlife have helped me better understand the truths about life.

At the time, my child mind couldn't fully comprehend the information they were showing me on the other side. However, the lessons stayed with me. Then, through a lifetime of reflection, I was able to integrate this knowledge into my consciousness in a way that I could explain to others. The first and most important truth I will share with you is this: earth is a school, and life is a journey of lessons. Life is made up of continual sunrises and sunsets, summers and winters, high tides and low tides. We cannot stop these cycles, but we can learn to roll with them and master the dance of seasons. This book explores that dance through the lens of my life's journey.

❀ ❀ ❀

Did my near-death experience induce my journey to becoming a professional spiritual medium? Yes and no.

The truth is that I saw spirits from as young an age as I can remember. However, I never understood intellectually or spiritually what was happening; it just was. Growing up, I lived with my family near a grove with many small animals, so there was an opportunity to see loss and death in the natural world often. Although seeing dead animals would always make me sad, I was never afraid because I vividly remember seeing animal figures floating above their physical bodies, and I knew they were okay. I also regularly saw angels at the end of my bed—they looked almost dimmed but were undeniably heavenly lights. (I later learned that *dimming* their bright light was necessary when they visited our world so as not to scare us.)

Spirit communication is a gift passed down in my family. My mother had this ability too. Along with other instances, whenever she shared with us her dreams about the family, they were always accurate. However, my mother was afraid of her gift because she didn't want to be seen as crazy. After all, she had been disbelieved, forcibly confined, and medicated for it before. So she only spoke of it within our family and didn't share it with anyone else. My sister, instead of being afraid of her gift, embraced it and used it to help others. She developed a keen interest in energy-healing techniques and using her intuitive abilities to assist in emotional healing that helps to mend the body's physical ailments. My brother could also communicate with spirits when he was a child. Unfortunately, as he grew older, he found it increasingly overwhelming and wanted to distance himself from this ability. Despite his efforts, he could not push it away, and this struggle created a challenging journey for him.

So, while I have been an empath in tune with the spirit world for as long as I can remember, my near-death experience "pierced the veil" for me profoundly. Nothing would ever be as it once was, despite all my best attempts at denial and living a "normal" life, I was unmistakably cracked, never to be the same again. But there are ways of being whole with all our cracks. In the centuries-old Japanese art of Kintsugi, broken pottery is repaired with precious metals, resulting in an even more exquisite piece than the original, with all its cracks highlighted. In the same way, we, too, can transform our broken human hearts into divine gold and shine brighter than we ever could have imagined. And this isn't just something I *think*; it's something I was *shown* by the lights that greeted me in the dark on that happy-turned-tragic day.

INTEGRATION MOMENT
Bringing Your Darkness to the Light

Pause now. Breathe. This is your first Integration Moment, designed to help you process all that you've learned in this chapter. You may want to put this book down and come back to it when you have the space to meditate and journal uninterrupted for 15 to 30 minutes.

We've all had our "cracks" in life, we've all experienced heartbreaking grief and grievances, and we have all been shattered along the way. We tend to bury these tragic events deep in the darkness, but true healing occurs when we bring them to the light. Our darkest paths are our greatest assets; we must walk them fully.

I invite you to take some time to journal about this chapter's theme and how it applies to your life, guided by any of the following prompts of your choosing:

- What was your first "crack"—your earliest memory of suffering?
- Which experiences have facilitated positive changes in your life?

- What has been your greatest lesson? Why?

- In what ways have you transformed your human grief into divine gold in your life so far?

- What people, places, and situations in your childhood planted a seed in your soul that grew into a complete understanding of the lesson you were meant to learn?

Chapter Exercise

Knowledge is wonderful, but many of us need practical advice to put it into action! That's what these chapter exercises are for. There are many exercises that can open you up to valuable introspection. In this book, I'll share my favorite, easiest exercises to help guide you into self-reflection.

Affirmations are phrases that support the manifestation of experiences, beliefs, or feelings. If you keep thinking about negative things, you are "affirming" to your subconscious mind and the universe that you want *more* of that. Creating positive affirmations that focus on what you *do* want to feel or experience helps bring them into reality. Affirmations can create an internal environment for your soul that reaches beyond your thinking into self-knowledge and healing.

It is simple to create your own affirmations. Write down short, positive statements in the present tense and in the first person "I." You don't want to affirm "I will be a whole, loving person" or "I don't have negative thoughts anymore." The first affirmation keeps your good in the future rather than the now. In the second statement, your subconscious skips over the "don't" and focuses only on the negativity, which is the opposite of what you want.

- For this exercise, write a list of 30 affirmations that focus on your healing and the positive things you see (or wish to see) in yourself.

- Every day, choose one or two affirmations to focus on. You might write them down and put them where you will see them often.

- Repeat your affirmations to yourself in your mind or aloud as often as you remember. Every time you have a negative thought, follow it up with one of your positive affirmations.

- Set aside time daily to say your list of affirmations. Make sure there are no interruptions. If you catch yourself having negative thoughts during the process, take a few deep breaths and begin again.

- Here are some examples of positive affirmations to get you started:

  + I bring personal empowerment to all situations.

  + I am worthy, lovable, and capable of healing.

  + I am filled with the essence of all that is good and right.

  + I am whole and complete just as I am.

Don't expect to see immediate results with affirmations. It takes 26 days to begin the challenging task of reprogramming your mind. In fact, new studies show that it can take up to 63 days of repetition to complete a significant enterprise. Be patient with yourself and with the process.

CHAPTER 2

The Room of Hearts' Desires

"Breathe slowly and stop screaming, Susie," the lights continued to say in their gentle, warm way.

I was still attempting to wriggle out of the freezer, but I was growing tired, and the lights felt more and more welcoming. Sensing my growing trust, they slowly came closer to me. I couldn't deny that their loving radiance felt so nurturing and safe, like a mother, which is all I wanted this whole time: my mommy.

The lights presented themselves as a surrogate, and I eventually surrendered to their embrace; I was so tired after such a long fight. As my mind lost consciousness, my soul began to feel as if I were dreaming. I will never forget this feeling of being guided by forces that were assisting me in crossing over. It was as gentle as a child being led by their mommy. And then suddenly, I was in a new, unfamiliar place—the spirit realm!

What's going on? Where am I? Where's my mommy? These thoughts ran through me as I experienced the sensation of being in another place, in another space and time. For a moment, the fear from the freezer lingered with me, and I started rocking my body in an attempt to comfort myself. But immediately, the lights somehow wrapped around me, offering me the warmest embrace I had ever felt. I knew I was safe.

The words *I know you love me more than anything* kept repeating in my head, but the thought didn't originate from me. I knew suddenly that the lights loved me so much. It was like they had injected it into my soul as a calming mantra. From that point forward, the fear vanished, and a sense of peace came over me. I was still young, I was still me, and I still wanted my mommy, but when the warmth of the lights enveloped me, I became knowing, calm, and curious. I became ready for what lay ahead.

With the lights by my side, I began to take in this new place. I found myself at the bottom of a set of stairs, and I just knew I needed to get to the top. I had no idea how I would do that, however, because I felt what I can only describe as "Jell-O-y"—unable to move my body in the way I was used to, even though I looked like me physically. But as soon as I began to wonder how I would get up the stairs, I found myself there. My thoughts seemed to manifest instantly.

At the top of the stairs, I found myself in a circular, Greco-Roman-style room. I didn't know anything about architectural style at that young age, of course, but today I can place it. At the time, I just knew it looked so foreign and enchanting. To say it was beautiful would be the understatement of my lifetime.

"Where am I?" I asked, full of wonder. At this point, I suddenly understood that the lights still brightly glowing at my side were angels. They gazed at me with huge smiles, and a sense of knowing and belonging washed over me. It felt like they had cleansed my soul with their love.

"You're in the Room of Hearts' Desires," they said.

I'll use the word *said,* but what's closer in accuracy is that they *sang.* I quickly learned that when angels speak, words and music come out simultaneously—without their having to open their mouths. They speak through their souls telepathically, and their language and music radiate pure healing and love. The cadence of their voices is very particular; the closest thing I can liken it to on earth is the whale song. I can't completely explain why or how the angels share the way they do—all I can tell you is the beauty of their voices is the most exquisite sound I have ever heard, and it feels like medicine. Just as hearing a symphony of whales brings us into harmony with Mother Earth's rhythms, hearing the angelic music of the soul brings us into harmony with the nature of the Divine.

I don't have words for the beauty and awe I felt and saw there. I was illuminated by radiant light and stunning colors moving all around me. My surroundings burst with greenery and flowers so bright and alive they vibrated. It almost looked like an unrealized live painting to me and so unlike anything I had ever seen in my short lifetime. It was so unbelievable, vibrant, and happy. I felt like I had entered a new world brimming with excitement and pos-sibilities, and my soul was able to touch all this majestic beauty effortlessly.

The circular room was full of large columns, many of which were broken, like an ancient ruin, and they didn't seem to attach to anything, as there was no ceiling or walls. The room was completely open to the bright light of the celestial skies above. There were perfectly clear crystals everywhere, including floating above me. One crystal in particular seemed to be the most important—a gigantic, gorgeous quartz pyramid with fluid-like walls.

Being a curious kid, I reached into the giant crystal with my hand. Then I tried to get fully inside it but couldn't, and I realized that was because I wasn't meant to. To this day, it still makes me cry to think of it. It seemed to be a gateway of some kind, and I didn't have access to cross it. I could see the outlines of bodies, but no faces, moving within the crystal and knew that they were souls. On the other side, I could see movement beyond just bodies—not clouds, not water, but some other depth.

Suddenly, I realized that once a soul passed beyond the crystal, they could not return to their previous form. The souls I could see had already crossed over from their most recent lifetime, and I knew that some of them were people I loved. I didn't know who they were exactly, just that I loved them, and it was a heartwarming feeling.

I began to sense, then, that there were others on my side of the alluring crystal that I could actually interact with. People walked across the room with bodies that were so floppy, it was as if they might dissolve into liquid at any second, like butter melting on a pan. They had other figures with them who appeared to be their loved ones, guiding them. No one told me that, but I felt that deep love between them.

"Are you okay?" I asked one of them, concerned.

"Oh yes, I'm just not used to my ethereal body yet!" They flashed a huge smile at me and continued moving along. I remember wondering what exactly an "ethereal body" was, but I knew my body felt the same way. I instinctively knew they had just crossed over and were being transported to another space I hadn't yet reached.

Lessons Contained within the Well

With the bright skies above me and souls around me, I peered below and saw a dark abyss that looked like a well. But despite its darkness, I didn't feel afraid of it in the slightest. When I say it looked like a well, that's what it looked like to my four-almost-five self. It's important to note that this entire experience was filtered through the brain of my child self, and I remember it the same today as I did then. I found myself just *knowing* some things, but I wasn't all-knowing. Whatever I was meant to know that a child carries the capacity to understand was downloaded into me effortlessly and instantly. The far more complex things I would learn to make sense of later in life.

Dr. Raymond Moody—who coined the term "near-death experience (NDE)" in his 1975 book *Life After Life,* and whom I studied under to receive my doctorate of divinity degree—later told me that my description could be "the tunnel" that so many near-death experiencers describe. The dark tunnel has been described in many different ways, such as a cave, a well, an enclosure, a funnel, a vacuum, a void, a sewer, a valley, or a cylinder. I can never be 100 percent sure if it was the famed tunnel, but I can say with certainty that the feeling of "eternity" as I gazed upon it was undeniable. I remember looking at this circular well at the bottom of the room, then up again to the circular opening at the top of the building, and just knowing. My young human self didn't know the word *eternity* in the slightest, but my ethereal spirit self undoubtedly understood that this was somewhere eternal, going on and on, forever and ever—and I got the sense that I might be as well.

I wonder what's down there. Once again, my thought became an instant reality, and I found myself right next to the ledge of the well. The three angels stood by me, infusing me with comfort and love. Soft music played in the background like the gentle swaying of tree branches on a breezy day.

I felt invited by some force bigger than me to peer inside the well. When I looked down, I saw movement in the dark. Focusing my eyes, I saw millions of words and sentences intermingling like they were swirling around in a blender. I couldn't yet read, but I knew I saw words and understood I was witnessing something miraculous. With today's perspective, I can say they looked almost like endless strands of DNA dancing about each other.

"What is that?" I asked in wonderment.

"Those are the heart's desires of every living soul."

Even though I didn't fully understand, I felt the depth of emotion behind the words my angelic tour guides were saying to me. Observing all the hopes, dreams, heartbreaks, and prayers of all the people on the planet mixing together in the well, I felt we were all one. I *knew* we were, even though I didn't understand the implications of that truth.

In the human world, we experience ourselves as separate, individualistic, and divided—but the bigger truth behind the curtain is that we all think and dream and hope and suffer and pray alike, making up a unified collective consciousness where every thought we have and every action we take affects the whole. We are all drops of water in the same ocean, ebbing and flowing with the totality.

It's no wonder that "treat others the way you would like to be treated" is a directive in nearly every religion that exists. If I am mean to you, I am mean to me; if I refuse to forgive you, I refuse to forgive me; if I am loving to you, I am loving to me. At that moment, I understood "oneness" for the first time.

"Do you make all of those wishes come true?" I asked. Somewhere deep inside of me, my soul knew these people were desperate and in need of answers. My heart hoped the answer to my question was a resounding yes!

"No, Susie, not all of them," they replied. "Sometimes, what people desire the most isn't good for them."

Well, I had heard that before. It was one of my mother's go-to statements—one I didn't particularly appreciate hearing. After my natural, childlike responses to being told no to more candy or sleeping in her bed, she always said, "You don't always get what you want, Susie, because it might not be good for you." And just as my mom denied my wishes sometimes to protect me, the spirit world hears and empathizes with every single one of our prayers but sometimes must deny them for our own greatest good. What the human ego wants isn't always what the soul's expansion needs.

The angels, of course, knew that explaining this profound concept by using my mom's language would feel safe and familiar to me, and it did, especially coming from such loving, beautiful light beings. The spirit world intentionally shows us things and explains concepts to us in familiar ways for that very reason—so that we understand them! My experiences as a professional evidential medium confirm this. When spirits want to communicate with us, the manner in which they do so won't be foreign to us. They come as we understand them so that we are not afraid. From the outset of this visit, I was shown angels from the spirit world because angels made sense based on my Catholic upbringing. At that stage in my life, I knew angels were loving, kind, and trustworthy. Therefore, that is what I was shown as a means to comfort me and lessen my fear. It's ultimately a loving act of protection, which is no surprise because angels are pure love.

Because the angels explained this lesson in a way that felt validating and affirming to me based on my life experience up until that point, I trusted and carried it with me from that moment forward. But still, I didn't understand why. Why wouldn't they help people whenever they prayed? Were some people better than others? Were they going to grant my deep desire to be back with my mommy?

Near-death experience narratives usually relay that the person did not want to return to their human body, but that was not the case for me. As is typical, I was no longer afraid or suffering in the afterlife. It felt loving and wonderful, and I enjoyed it very much. Still, I deeply felt that I wanted my mommy.

Most of the children I work with today who have experienced visitations to the other side have shared similar feelings with me of wanting to come back. Why? Most children are still highly in tune with the spirit world yet connected to the joys of human life. They are hopefully living the best of both worlds. They are whole, pure, and happy—until the more challenging realities of life eventually find them, and the cracks begin.

Conversely, adults *don't* want to return because they know firsthand that life is tough—they're already chipped at best and shattered at worst. They are exhausted from the burdens of Earth school. So the pure, whole bliss they encounter on the other side feels like a reprieve they aren't willing to trade easily!

Yet, as I just learned, my deep desire to return to my mommy didn't necessarily mean that wish would be granted. First, the angels wanted to answer my inquiry as to why we cannot always get what we want. Therefore, we needed to take a walk on the Yellow Brick Road.

INTEGRATION MOMENT
Reframing Human Rejection as Divine Redirection

No, we can't always get what we want! In future chapters, we will delve into the why of this matter. For now, I invite you to view our perceived rejections in life as Divine redirection. Integrate this lesson by taking some time to meditate and journal on any of the following prompts of your choice:

- What are some things in your life that you thought you needed but didn't ever receive? What feelings does this elicit for you?

- Describe a point in your life when not getting something you really wanted worked out for the best. How did that rejection ultimately help you grow and redirect you toward a better path? What would have happened if you'd gotten what you thought you wanted?

- Can you recall times when you "just knew" something but didn't act on it, and it came to light that you should have listened? List a few consequences of not listening to the wisdom of your intuition.

- What are some times you did act on your intuitive knowledge? List those good results in your journal.

Chapter Exercise

Music is very healing to your soul and raises your vibration. The angels speak to us through their music, which helps us understand why music is so healing to humans on a universal level. Just as the angels use music to heal others, so can you.

- Think of what music soothes your soul. Why? This would be good music to listen to while you read, journal, or meditate.

- Take time to move with the music you love. Make a point to close your eyes and allow the sounds to resonate in your energy.

- While you dance or listen to music, think of times you've felt "oneness" before, times when you were connected to everything. Think of moments in your life when you *just knew* something, like it was *downloaded* into your brain.

- Write down the feelings you experienced during this exercise and how they impacted you. Are you peaceful and relaxed or feeling exhausted?

CHAPTER 3

The Reason for Life's Challenges

What is the meaning of life? We have all asked ourselves this age-old question at one point or another. For some of us, it's an occasional passing thought on hard days. For others, it's the main thread of every single day. Regardless, we all have an instinct that tells us there must be more to life than material-world monotony.

From a human perspective, it's safe to say most of us think the meaning of life is to find peace, love, and joy. From a spiritual perspective, however, it's not quite that simple. When peace, love, and joy are what we consider to be "the point" of life, then we feel that we've failed when we don't feel these affirmative emotions. Considering the turbulent world we live in, this "failure" can happen quite often. If we're operating from this viewpoint, we can easily slip deeper and deeper into despair with each of life's inevitable roadblocks. What the spirit world taught me about the meaning of our human lives, and the reason for the challenges that weave throughout them, is a significant shift from this perspective: The meaning of human life is to expand our souls and cultivate self-love through our choices. Hardships are the most powerful fertilizer in which to do so.

For the love of God, please help me. Have you ever found yourself saying that? Many of us, at one time or another, have cried out to Spirit for help. Suffering is universal to the human experience, and contained within it is this feeling, the pull to surrender to something greater than ourselves.

At some point in our lives—and for some of us, at many points—we are *all* brought to our knees. It could be the death of a loved one, a divorce, the loss of a pet, a job loss, a devastating diagnosis, an abusive relationship or situation, or another life-altering event. Our darkest moments, when seen from a spiritual perspective, are when we attain our most profound soul growth. Within our dark nights of the soul, we are burdened with such intense despair that carrying on the way things have been becomes impossible. It's a change-or-be-changed moment. It's in these low human moments that we are propelled to search for our greater selves. Our obstacles are often our gateways to the Divine.

Certainly, the opportunity exists to learn and expand through joy as much as through pain. But when times are good, the majority of us simply do *not* take those giant leaps of faith required for actual soul growth. It's not impossible or unheard of, but it's an exception to the human experience. For most of us, striving for spiritual growth takes hitting rock bottom, whatever that looks like for us. Pain is our greatest motivator for change.

Just as the ocean will always have waves, life, too, will always have challenges. They ebb in and flow out. We don't know what each inward wave will bring with it, but we know it will bring something. It's not our job to try to lessen the waves but to become better surfers. During my journey through the afterlife, the angels showed me a more manageable approach to navigating the waves of our lives, provided we are willing to have trust.

The Pavers of the Yellow Brick Road

When I left the Room of Hearts' Desires, the angels led me into a new place and showed me a glistening, golden path, which reminded me of *The Wizard of Oz*. I dubbed it the "Yellow Brick Road," even though the bricks were more golden than yellow. The angels never gave me a proper name for this place, so that's how I refer to it to this day. I knew the angels had built this stunning path out of their pure love—and they had built it for us humans.

Many human souls were working hard to pave their own paths, separate from the golden road. I watched them walk toward a pyramid of golden pavers near the path, pull them from the bottom of the pile one by one, and lay them down to create their next step. As they pulled bricks from the bottom of the pyramid it became unbalanced, threatening to topple over like a game of Jenga in its final stages.

"What are they doing?" I asked the angels, concerned.

"They're acting through their free will, Susie, trying to lay their own paths."

The human souls thought it was their job to pave their own paths, but the ones they were trying so hard to create were continually crooked, bumpy, and broken. They felt distraught and defeated, completely unaware that an easier spirit-led way was already created for them. I watched them fall to their knees and plead, "For the love of God, please help me."

Once a soul cried out for help, angels would swoop in, take the paver the person had just laid down, and put it back where it belonged at the base of the pyramid to stabilize it. And then the angels would take a paver from the top of the pyramid and start paving the path for the person again, the way it was meant to be. They seemed to be correcting human errors.

"What does this mean?" I asked.

"We are the true pavers," the angels said. "You are not. All you have to do is walk your path."

"But how do you know if you're walking your path right?"

"Because we're always blessing or blocking your path, guiding you toward what's meant for you. Make no mistake, you can get through a block, though battered and bruised, if you choose. But the better choice is to trust us, accept 'what is,' and shift your path. If there's still a block, you make another choice and shift again. Then if there's still a block, you shift yet again. We will pave the path for you—all you have to do is walk it, paying attention to both the blocks and the openings."

Even though much of what they said didn't make sense to me then, I clearly understood that they were in charge. "You were created by Spirit," they said, reading my mind, "and we love you and want more for you. You think you know what's best for you, but we know what's best for you. So when you release the thought patterns of what you think you should be doing and put your trust in us, your path will be easier."

Later in my life, I realized that the pyramid of golden pavers represented our life journey and pulling bricks represented the choices we make. Choosing to pull from the bottom, thereby unbalancing the pyramid, represented an imbalanced life journey. Balance is crucial in all we do; otherwise, addictions and significant difficulties find us.

As humans with egotistic brains, we keep making choices that aren't good for us because we think we know best. We place our trust in the visible world of matter, confident that we are the creators, the masters, and the ones in control. If we don't do it, no one will, right? But spirits showed me that this couldn't be further from the truth.

The spirit world is waiting for us to see that they are always here to help us. They are the lighthouses in the storms of our lives, but so many of us refuse to open our eyes to their guidance. More often than not, our ego gets in the way of asking the angels and our guides for help, and they will not interfere even when we are navigating through rough waters.

We have all experienced metaphorical doors slamming in our faces. We might've wanted something so badly and then an outside force swooped in and said, "No, this isn't for you—next!" Rejection is a difficult thing for our egos to cope with, but for our souls, it's simply a redirection to a better path for our spiritual growth. If the path is blocked, it's blocked for a reason, and we are meant to shift to another, more aligned direction.

This sounds easy enough—viewing our challenges as invitations to shift and bloom—but why is it such a difficult concept for us to really integrate? The spirit world is asking us to see roadblocks as redirects to a better path. Yet so many of us immediately start trying to figure out a way around them so we can continue in the same direction. When we think we can control every aspect of our lives, blocks seem to us like personal failures, and we can't have that! We want what we want when we want it, and society certainly celebrates that gritty human willpower. The angels are asking us instead to have faith in that which we cannot see, allowing the golden path they have paved for us to unfold.

With great warmth, the angels revealed to me that in our pursuit of success, we tend to prioritize "winning" above all else and, therefore, resort to pushing through obstacles. However, these challenges are not meant to be conquered forcefully. Instead, they are intended to be accepted and appreciated as valuable experiences, just as much as when we have a smooth and effortless journey. Essentially, both roadblocks and open paths serve as tools to keep us on track toward our goals. It's like the famous Quaker proverb says: "Proceed as way opens."

The angels told me we could step into our highest alignment on the golden path built specifically for us when we let go of control. "You see, Susie, what you run from chases you, and what you try to control, controls you," they explained. Reflecting honestly on our lives, we must ask ourselves: Where has running and controlling ever gotten us except into trouble? From a soul perspective, learning to trust in the spirit world, especially in the seemingly bad times, is the one and only ticket to the first-class human experience—and the fastest and most comfortable track to growing our souls and fulfilling the meaning of our lives.

What about Free Will?

With all this urging to let go of control and to hand the wheel of our lives over to Spirit, I'm sure free will is the big question on your mind right now. The angels told me that we absolutely, no-questions-asked have free will. Free will is *the point* of our human incarnations. We are here on earth, quite literally, to make choices to expand our souls. The growth is found *in* the choices we make.

Placing our trust in Spirit does not mean that everything is predestined for us, nor does it mean that everything will be effortless when we do so. What it does mean is that life becomes both more manageable and meaningful for us when we trust there is a spirit team guiding us—and we can better do what we are meant to do here.

Our spirit team consists of our soul group—all the souls, angels, and guides that we have chosen to support and help us on this journey. Our loved ones in the afterlife are familiar souls who have crossed over and maintain a connection with those they left behind, primarily motivated by love and the desire to offer comfort and presence. Angelic guides are spiritual beings who serve as messengers or protectors, guiding individuals throughout their earthly lives. These beings possess divine wisdom and provide guidance in accordance with a higher spiritual purpose. Angelic guides are separate entities with a broader cosmic purpose, while spirit guides are nonphysical entities or energies whose purpose is to provide guidance, protection, and wisdom to individuals on their life journey.

The groups of souls making up our spirit teams are standing by, ready to offer direction whenever we are in need. There is nothing special we must do to receive their guidance except ask. But because your free will cannot be interfered with, they can *only* intervene in your life when you have requested they do so.

To me, the common platitude "everything happens as it's supposed to" gives the impression that everything is predestined. This is not what I was shown during my near-death experience, nor in my decades working as a medium since. If everything were predestined, then our decisions would mean nothing, and the meaning of life would then become *meaningless*. This sacred, inviolable nature of our free will is why I believe that no one can offer *total* accuracy as a psychic reader. It would be difficult to tell people what their future holds when they can choose differently at any given moment.

At one time or another, we have all been brought to our knees in our life's most challenging moments, and in those moments, we get to *decide* what to do with that pain. As the saying goes, "You can grow bitter, or you can grow better." What I decide to do with the valleys of my life is my choice, just as what you choose to do with yours is your choice, and those choices determine the rate of our soul expansion. My life, for instance, has been rife with trauma, but I chose to transmute my darkness into light. I chose to become *more*, even though I had every reason to choose less.

We all have good reasons to feel victimized in this life, but when we make the conscious choice to be the victors of our circumstances, we truly grow on a soul level. We can choose not to grow from it all, absolutely. We can wallow for ages and cry, "Why me?!" We can choose to burrow into a hole, hide in our rooms, cover our heads, and not deal with life. We can even choose to kill ourselves and not face the pain of life any longer—that's how powerful our free will is. I have learned from the spirit world that our souls would not be happy with those decisions. But, the fact remains, free will *is* ours.

Our free will is crucial because it enables us to experience personal growth and transformation. Ultimately, each choice we make as individuals alters the course of our journey and leads us on a different path: this in turn changes the outcome of our experiences and growth potential.

Earth Is Our Soul's School

You might be wondering, Why would we even come here if the other side is so blissful? I have certainly asked myself that question, knowing what I know about the pure elation of the other side. But would you believe me if I told you that, as souls, we actually request to come here, pain and all? As we will see in the next chapter, we spend a lot of time preparing and planning to do so.

Just as we would not be able to see the light of the stars without the contrast of the deep black of space, our loving souls require contrast in order to be fully experienced, expressed, and seen. In this analogy, earth is the dark to our soul's light. That isn't to say life on earth doesn't hold exquisite joy and beauty; it does. But compared to our spiritual home, earth is no easy feat—and it's not meant to be. As souls in the spirit world, we want to come here despite the inevitable struggle because that is how we learn, grow, and experience ourselves. While the spirit world is all-knowing, it is not experiential.

Think of it this way: You can go to medical school for many, many years to become a heart surgeon. You can read every piece of educational literature available, sit in lectures by the world's best surgeons, and practice your skills extensively. You might have all the technical knowledge of how to do the surgery, but until you actually perform the surgery on a live, beating human heart, can you really say you have the understanding and experience of doing the surgery or call yourself a heart surgeon? No, you cannot. Similarly, in the spirit world, you can know everything there is to know about your pure love-and-light soul, but until you experience a place that contrasts that with pain and darkness, you can never truly master an understanding of yourself. The light needs the dark to experience itself. The cracks in life are actually where life's gold can be found.

What Happens to "Bad" People?

I realized I had one more question for the angels as I processed everything they relayed. I somewhat understood that our souls and lives on "the other side" were pure love and bliss, but we come to earth to learn through contrast. I somewhat understood we have free will to make choices and grow. These lessons would continue to make more sense as I went through my life journey. Still, as a four-almost-five-year-old, I was actively learning right and wrong in my own human life at the time, so I had to ask the burning question, "What happens to souls that use their free will to do bad things?"

The angels then showed me a scene of people being greeted into the afterlife with applause, acceptance, and love after their human lifetime. I watched the angels cheer, "Good job, you were so brave!" At that moment, there was no judgment whatsoever, no matter how they died or what they had done on this planet. They were praised for simply having the courage to come here in a physical body.

"So *nothing* happens to bad people?" Though I wasn't yet consciously aware that the abuse happening to me was wrong, I did understand that there were bad people in the world by this point in life. I also had a concept of heaven and hell by this time, courtesy of my Catholic upbringing, so this pure acceptance didn't quite make sense to me.

"There are no bad souls, Susie, because all souls are from the spirit realm! However, there are injured and broken humans, and those injured humans make broken, unhealthy, and sometimes *evil* choices. We embrace those who have struggled to make healthy choices in life, and they still must face the harm they have done on their journey. A golden rule in the spirit world is: What you give to others, so shall you experience!

"We take those souls to a place of healing, similar to what humans call a hospital. We help them bring light to the darkness they created for themselves and others while on the planet. They review and experience how they have made others feel in their most recent human journey. It is not a punishment but a way to commit to better choices in their next lifetime."

Evil is in the minds of man, not the souls of spirits! At the time, it seemed like a hard pill to swallow. However, as I grew more spiritually aware on my journey, I realized the value of healing over punishment. Now, I pray for the healing of all so that there are no more victims of the horrible atrocities that can and do happen to us.

The angels continued, "Once they are rejuvenated, we let them back into the soul groups that they belong to, and then they try again. . . ."

Soul groups? Just as I started to form the question in my soul, off we went!

INTEGRATION MOMENT
Challenges, Choices, Changes

Like seeds, we have the opportunity to grow when we are planted in dark soil. Our darkest paths can become our greatest assets—but it *is* a choice we must make to do so. Making conscious choices is critical because it is the most significant determiner of our journey on earth. As we progress in life, it's important to reflect on our choices and monitor our growth. Choosing any of the journaling prompts below, I encourage you to meditate and explore the lessons of this chapter.

- Describe a time you resisted a block in your life's path and tried to power through anyway. What was the result?

- Describe a time you accepted a block in the road and chose to shift in a new direction. What was the result?

- The angels told me, "What you run from chases you, and what you try to control, controls you." What do you run from? What do you try to control?

- Would you say, thus far in your life, you have chosen to grow bitter or to grow better?

- Many of us have had experiences with people who are considered morally reprehensible, whether directly or from a distance. However, the angels say no soul is inherently evil. How do you feel about this?

Chapter Exercises

There is no punishment on a soul level for our human mistakes. It can be very uncomfortable to know that someone who may have harmed you or your loved ones has a "free pass," but that is not a truth. What would be the ultimate goal in punishment, after all? Through healing and the ability to make new choices for our highest good, we break the cycle of harm.

- Make a list of the persons you have harmed. This list isn't for beating yourself up but for self-healing and reflection.

- Consider what happened in each situation. What were your own wounds? What led you to make these unhealthy choices?

- Have you made amends? Do this whenever possible except when doing so could cause injury to yourself or others. If this is the case, silent or living amends could be a possible choice, such as writing a letter you do not intend to mail and/or living in a way so as not to repeat those behaviors that caused harm.

The angels say that injured and broken humans make broken, unhealthy, and sometimes evil choices. That is why your own healing and self-care is absolutely vital. If you neglect yourself, then you'll keep hurting others even as you're trying to help.

The first step toward healing is self-awareness. To gain a better understanding of yourself, finish these sentences:

- I am my best self when . . .

- I become upset when . . .

- I am happiest when . . .

- I feel more open when . . .

- I am afraid when . . .
- One of the most important lessons I have learned is . . .
- I shut down when . . .
- One of my favorite memories is . . .
- The most difficult choices I have had to make were . . .
- I feel less than when . . .
- I can be myself only when . . .
- I can forgive myself when . . .
- I can forgive others when . . .
- I want to . . .
- I want to change these five things about myself . . .
- I want to understand . . .
- I will heal . . .
- I want to be more open to . . .
- I want to change my thinking in these areas . . .
- I admire people who . . .
- I feel I am enough when I . . .
- When others do wrong or unacceptable things, they should . . .
- I am making better choices today . . .

CHAPTER 4

Creating Our Soul Contracts

Have you ever felt like you unknowingly signed up somewhere for a Ph.D. in hardships? Or perhaps it's the opposite, and you've had a relatively smooth journey compared to most people you know. Whether you think you enrolled for the earth-on-easy-mode experience or the extreme master class, you *did*.

As discussed in the last chapter, the choices we make from our free will and the growth that stems from them are the point of our human incarnations. However, the next portion of my afterlife tour taught me that our free will doesn't just apply to our time spent as humans. It also applies to the time we spend *planning* our human lifetimes when we are on the other side.

While not every detail of our existence is pre-planned—because what would be the point in that?—we *do* determine the general lessons we want to experience, as well as the level of difficulty based on the stage of growth our soul is in at the time. Think of it as enrolling for the classes you want in college, but every choice you make throughout the course of the semester will impact the final results.

The Room of Knowledge

As the angels and I left the Yellow Brick Road, I found myself in a huge room like a vast hallway that expanded endlessly throughout time—it had a beginning but no apparent end. Crystals floated everywhere, and I felt a very high vibration of energy coursing all around me. There were many souls in the room, filling it with a lively chatter as they reviewed and discussed an array of holographic-like memory books. The souls looked sheer, almost as if you could see through them, yet they were still three-dimensional. Everything in this room seemed to sparkle, float, and vibrate, and my young self was enchanted.

"What is *this* place?" I asked.

"This, Susie, is the Room of Knowledge, where souls make decisions for their highest growth in their next incarnation."

Later in my life and spiritual journey, I learned of what many call the Akashic Records. While I still don't relate to that terminology, it is the same concept as what I experienced: a room full of all the details of our many lifetimes—past, present, and future.

As I observed the Room of Knowledge with childlike wonderment, information was being downloaded into my child self for future understanding. The angels showed me that upon our physical deaths, after being welcomed and congratulated for our brave journey, we experience a life review. We are shown our lessons through virtual-like memory books, including the dark and difficult circumstances during our lifetime. Our loving angels counsel us through our journey and help us understand that everything that happens to us, even the seemingly negative, has deep meaning for our souls and others. Each memory that flashes forward from the book has a profound meaning for our souls. To offer us a clearer understanding of the situations that we could have handled better, we experience these memories through others' perspectives, as if we've stepped into their emotional bodies. We *feel* the way we made them feel, not for the purposes of punishment but for the opportunity to learn from our mistakes and inform the curriculum we choose for our next lifetime.

Looking back, I believe our all-knowing higher self brings these memories forward to help us plan for our next phase of soul growth. The higher self is an elevated aspect of our consciousness, embodying greater wisdom, connection to one's true nature, and spiritual enlightenment in the afterlife. It is the part of our soul that stays behind to help guide us while the rest of our soul goes on to the human plane.

Once we recognize a specific lesson that we'd like to improve upon, that desire is entered into our soul's contract for our upcoming incarnation. (We are automatically "enrolled," so to speak.) For example, suppose that in their most recent lifetime, a person chooses to end their own life. During their review process, they may seek a deeper understanding of how their choice impacted others. Then in their new soul contract for their next incarnation, they may choose to have an experience where someone close to them is suicidal. They won't know the finer details of who will feel suicidal or whether they will act on that feeling. Still, the general lesson *will* be experienced somehow, some way, in that next lifetime.

Our soul contracts include difficult experiences that we consciously choose so that we can experience all sides of a situation, understand the lessons in totality, and develop compassion from direct, firsthand experience. This is the true meaning of karma, which has nothing to do with retribution and everything to do with education. It's not a punishment from some outside judgmental force but a means of soul evolution. There's no guilt or shame in it, only love and healing.

"Are you certain?" I telepathically heard a guide say to a soul actively planning its next incarnation. "Are you sure you feel you can go through *all* that pain in one lifetime?"

"Yes, I do feel I can," the soul replied. "I've been through many lifetimes; I am certain my soul can achieve this for my greatest growth! My soul has the desire to learn *these* lessons now . . ."

"Are you sure, dear? Maybe it's a bit too much all at once, and you should reconsider . . ."

"No, I can do it!" the soul said, determinedly, seemingly intent on receiving that Ph.D. in hardship I mentioned.

I found it interesting that the guide was discouraging such a challenging path. Sensing my curiosity, the angels explained, "We are discouraging this because we don't want this soul to feel overwhelmed to the point that they give up. We don't want life to get too defeating because they may feel they have no choice but to forfeit their human journey and the lessons they have chosen to learn. But souls have the final say when it comes to plotting their lives."

Today, I am relatively clear that a similar dissuasive conversation occurred between me and my spirit guides. Sometimes I think, *If I had only listened, life would have had fewer hardships and possibly have been a little more pleasant.* However, like many of us, I am determined; therefore, I chose the Ph.D.

The Types of Soul Contracts

There are two types of contracts that help us achieve the goals of spiritual soul growth: Karmic and dharmic.

Karmic and dharmic contracts are your soul's agreement before you come here to fulfill your present journey's intentions. Karma means the balancing and resolving of soul difficulties such as fear, betrayal, harm, and so on. As we evolve, we make mistakes using our free will as our decision-makers, and karmic soul contracts offer us the opportunity to grow and learn. Your highest integrity may not have been a part of these choices; therefore, you have chosen to return to this dimension and resolve the "misunderstanding" for your soul.

Dharmic contracts are more positive and gentle. Dharma is thought to be any lesson that is beyond this present lifetime's intended soul lesson. It is less about the individual's soul and more about raising the frequency of the planet. Dharma helps to increase collective consciousness and the individual's soul consciousness all in one swoop.

New Souls and Old Souls

Have you ever been called an "old soul" or know someone who radiates that energy? This concept really does exist in the spirit realm. An old soul, also called an advanced soul, is someone who has had many lifetimes. A new soul means new to experiencing this planet or, at the very least, one who has not been here often.

For clarity purposes, I'd like to note that being an old soul does not necessarily equate to being a wise soul, nor does being a new soul equate to being an unwise one.

In my personal experiences, I have met individuals who were considered old souls but made unwise choices or had challenges with soul growth, just as I have met individuals who were considered new souls but displayed great wisdom and personal growth. Regardless of the depth of their soul evolution, "souls always are and always will be."

In one of my mediumship training courses later in life, the teacher explained to us that new souls create soul contracts with many intense experiences—such as extreme poverty, trauma, loss, or disability—to grow at a rapid pace. Even though it didn't quite make sense to me, I listened intently. But as the teacher continued speaking, Spirit started stirring inside of me, infusing me with knowledge. "Raise your hand, raise your hand, take the mic!" I kept hearing Spirit say.

As a relative newbie in this class, I was thinking, *No, no, no, Are you kidding me?!* Interrupting a reputable teacher in the middle of a lecture was the last thing on my mind!

But Spirit wouldn't let up, getting louder and louder in my head, "Take the mic, take the mic!"

Reluctantly, I raised my hand and asked to speak. "This is actually backward," I said. Then my download from Spirit came pouring out. "Most new souls wouldn't be able to handle the intense pain associated with that type of life. They would find it too challenging and forfeit their human journey. In actuality, those difficult journeys are for the most advanced souls. They choose to incarnate into those circumstances for their own soul growth and the greater good's expansion."

The Buddhists call this kind of advanced soul a bodhisattva. Once full enlightenment is reached for themselves, a bodhisattva chooses to forgo an eternity of Nirvana to instead keep returning to the human plane to assist and inspire the rest of us in our journeys. Indeed, advanced souls come back to earth in various forms to remind us of our soul's essence. Sometimes we call them "earth angels"—they might be strangers who say something that stirs our soul in passing or whose presence somehow prompts more compassion or inspiration within us. Whatever it is, the interactions with these people feel somehow divine. And they are divine—we need these positive soul reminders on our human journeys.

As humans, we are often driven by our egoic minds, and we tend to default to a lack of gratitude and to focusing too much on our own self. However, when we see someone else in a difficult situation, we embrace compassion and humility, and then our love takes over. These old souls come here to stimulate those spiritual traits inside us, ultimately helping align us to the highest paths we intended for our soul's growth. In doing so, these souls, in turn, align with their own soul's evolution.

When Spirit was done speaking through me, reality set in. I was nervous about what the course instructor would say. But to my surprise, she gracefully announced to the class, "What just came out of your mouth, Susan, was gold."

Soul Groups

On the subject of earth angels, I want to share a powerful experience I had many years ago. One day, while my mom and I were leaving the assisted living facility where she lived, I noticed a woman. She appeared to be in her mid-80s and was walking down the hallway with her husband. We looked up at each other across the hall, and in that instant my soul was drawn to her like a magnet.

"Oh my God, I've missed you! I've missed you so much!" I said, walking swiftly to her.

"Oh my goodness," she replied. "I know you, and I've missed you too!"

We started hugging and crying and continued to share our souls, speaking aloud about how much we had missed each other. It was overwhelming, beautiful, and strange. I remember my mom and the woman's husband looking at us with confusion and uneasiness. I cried when we parted, deeply devastated to leave her, and she felt the same.

The connection was so strong; I have never felt anything like that again in my life. I felt like my soul knew her, and she was part of me. It was the most extraordinary experience and soul connection. My words cannot do it justice. I didn't even know her name, but I have grieved that woman ever since. I don't think *soulmate* explains it— it went beyond that. The experience left me feeling loved yet confused and alone all at once. Whoever this woman actually *was*, the soul bond was so unbelievably intense, it was as if she was a reflection of my soul, and I've missed her terribly every day since.

Have you ever met someone for the first time but felt in your bones like you have known them for much, much longer? Well, there's a high chance in those soul-stirring situations that you actually *have* known them for longer— perhaps even forever—as part of your soul group.

In the Room of Knowledge, I saw the souls about to incarnate receiving guidance from angels as well as their soul group members. I learned that these clusters of souls decided long ago to learn their spiritual lessons with each other through their reincarnations on earth. I watched many groups of these soul families making intricate life plans together, and it was evident that they had done this countless times, saying things like, "In this lifetime, I'll do this to learn this, and you'll do that to learn that, and I'll step in during this particular time in your life," and so on. If one of our soul group members wants a break from the earth plane for a bit, they still serve on our spirit team as a guide.

When you connect with a person many times in your life, know that these connections are not a coincidence. They are karmic connections, contracted by you in the Room of Knowledge, for your personal soul growth. The purpose is to learn something about yourself and for them to do the same.

Suddenly, I started seeing these soul groups vanish from the room. "What just happened to them? Where did they go?" I asked.

"They went to the Waiting Station," explained the angels. "And now it's time for you to go there, too, Susie."

Soul Growth

The angels didn't share with me the details of my soul contracts while I was in the Room of Knowledge. They did tell me that going back into my body meant I would have a more challenging life, but also that it would be worth it. It would serve to both grow my soul and help others grow theirs.

And they were right—a return to my human life was signing me up for years of trauma. But the Room of Knowledge helped me put my "painful" experiences into context, and it became clear to me *why* I chose various challenges in my own human incarnations. I have learned that my deep pain inspired the necessary healing and growth that ultimately allowed me to serve others the way I do now.

Take, for example, my sorrow of not being able to experience carrying and birthing a baby. Having the birthing experience had always been my number one desire in this lifetime. I endured five surgeries, along with three attempts at in vitro fertilization (IVF), to try to conceive without success. It felt like my body had betrayed me. It was one of the deepest losses of my life, and I've experienced *a lot* of loss in my many years here! I kept thinking at the time, *Why would my soul want this? Why would my soul decide on such a trauma?* Even years later, after creating my beautiful family through adoption, the inability to ever feel a baby moving inside of my body has remained a significant heartbreak in my life.

However, I know that I did indeed agree to make this contract, because my father's spirit came to me after he died and took me back to the Room of Hearts' Desires. After my visit, upon the return to my physical body, I heard him saying to me over and over, "Your heart's desire, your heart's desire, your heart's desire . . ."

I was lying in my bed, his words ringing through my head, and suddenly I began experiencing the physical sensations of giving birth. It wasn't like a dream—I felt the experience quite profoundly. I felt movement in my stomach and every sensation. When the painful experience ended, I got out of bed, clenching my stomach, sweating and sobbing. And then it all stopped—the experience was over as quickly as it had come.

"This was my gift to you." My father knew my heart's greatest desire was to experience childbirth and so gave me this beautiful gift from his soul.

Many years after my first visit to the Room of Hearts' Desires, my father reminded me of the lesson I learned then, that what we want the most isn't always best for our soul's growth. Simultaneously, he gave me a simulation of my heart's greatest desire, creating healing for me on a soul level that I wasn't even aware I still needed. Ultimately, this allowed me to release the unconscious grief that was *still* deeply stirring inside my heart. I now knew my pain had a powerful spiritual purpose in my life. This contractual "limitation" paved the way to the amazing experience my soul was meant to have during this lifetime: adopting two children and being a guardian of a third.

One day, not long after receiving the sad news that I wouldn't be able to have biological children, my broken heart was lifted by a phone call. A sweet baby girl was about to be born, and her birth parents wanted to help us create our family. The gift of this news was like a warm embrace for my soul.

When our baby girl arrived, I walked into a hospital nursery filled with at least 30 other babies. Without hesitation, I walked straight to her bassinet. I could feel her energy calling me, and I recognized her soul and knew she was meant to be mine. The moment the nurse said, "Congratulations, Mommy," tears of pure joy streamed down my face. I finally felt all was right in my world.

Years later, after many failed adoptions, I still yearned to expand our family. I waited with hope and love for another precious baby to arrive. She was taking so long, and I feared she might never come. I just wanted another baby to love; no, my soul *needed* another baby.

One day, I was driving in my car, crying over this tremendous loss. Suddenly, I heard my future child as loud as if she were in the car with me, "Don't cry, Mama. I am coming to you. I just haven't been born yet, but I'll be here in two weeks."

I heard it so clearly; it permeated my very essence and still gives me that same profound feeling to this day. The message was so powerful, and I knew it was real. This was my baby; this was my soul family.

A week and a few days later, we received a call about a baby who would be born any day. Two weeks from the day I heard her in the car, my daughter was in my arms! I now know that my adopted children were contracted to be with me. I was meant to be their mommy, to nurture and love them on this planet; they were meant to be my children. However, my body couldn't carry them during this lifetime, so they had to find a different path to get to me. Not being able to conceive was the greatest grief of my life, but it also brought me the greatest gifts of my life, and I would never change that journey for anything in the world.

Today, I work with many people who are stuck deep in the throes of grief over their inability to birth children. Because of my own soul healing and firsthand experiences with this issue, I am now able to offer them sincere compassion, inspiration, and eventual understanding of this challenging aspect of their journey.

Our compassion truly blossoms when we understand something directly, and that's what our soul-contracted life lessons are all about. We know all this while preparing for our next life journey in the Room of Knowledge. But in the Waiting Station that I was about to be led into next, we begin the process of trading the *knowledge* we have in the spirit world for the firsthand *experience* of that knowledge in the human world.

INTEGRATION MOMENT
Reviewing Your Soul Contracts

If you've ever felt like you just know someone, something, or someplace, you are most likely remembering some aspect of your soul contracts. These soul memories are impossible to ignore, even if they seem to carry little human logic. Choose any of the prompts below to try to reconnect with the soul contracts you made before coming into this current lifetime.

- Do you ever get the sense that something in your life was planned or contracted by you before incarnating here? What lesson do you think you intended to learn from it?

- If you had to describe the theme of all the lessons you've learned in your life thus far, what would it be?

- Based on the description in this chapter, do you consider yourself to be a new soul, an old soul, or somewhere in between? Why do you feel that way?

- Who do you know in this lifetime that you feel is undoubtedly a part of your soul family and why?

- Maya Angelou famously said, "People will forget what you said, people will forget what you did, but people will never forget how you made them feel." The life review process seems to confirm this. If you had to imagine your life review right now, how do you think you have made people feel over the course of your lifetime?

Chapter Exercises

The purpose of soul contracts is to be accountable for your soul choices prior to coming to this plane of existence. We incarnate into this world and consciousness to carry out our intended missions for soul expansion—this then helps us to achieve a higher level of soul growth and to *evolve* our soul consciousness. Because of our choices, we can bring happiness or suffering. Karmic cycles are repeating patterns or situations caused by our actions and choices.

- What are some of your karmic patterns and cycles?

- What areas of your life are so repetitive that every time you think, *This is now over,* lo and behold, you encounter it again?

- What positive karma have your choices created? List as many as you can.

- What negative karma have your choices created? List as many as you can.

- When have you felt a need to clean something up in your life and ignored that feeling?

Remember the karmic connections you contracted in the Room of Knowledge for your personal growth. Each time you connect with a person from your soul group, the goal is to learn and grow on a soul level from these encounters.

- List karmic connections that you feel you contracted that have been difficult for your soul.

- List karmic connections that you feel you contracted to bring happiness and peace to your journey.

- How can you heal these repeated patterns?
  - ✦ Have you forgiven yourself?
  - ✦ Have you let go of the anger or resentment?
  - ✦ Are you carrying fear?
  - ✦ Are you being mindful of your actions, deeds, words, and thoughts?

A dharmic life is knowing you have a higher purpose. That higher purpose is to be spiritually conscious of how you live your life. The dharmic life goal is fulfilling your divine potential and continuously creating situations that help you move toward it.

- In what ways are you fulfilling your dharmic contracts?
- How are you of service to others and the whole of consciousness?
- List ways in which your journey has inspired and helped to heal or support others.
- What does your heart tell you is your true purpose?

CHAPTER 5

Among the "Dead"

Nearly all creation stories suggest that water is the origin of life. That's difficult to dispute when you consider that most living beings have large amounts of water in their bodies, that we need water not only to function but also to survive, and that, as any modern scientist will tell you, the presence of water is the prerequisite for life. At my next stop, the Waiting Station, I was shown that our souls enter the human body through water. And that's precisely how I returned to mine.

When I left the Room of Knowledge, I looked around and saw that I was in the middle of an enormous field, all by myself for the first time in this near-death experience. I wasn't afraid; I sat on the lush green grass, picking daisies, and watched many happy dogs running through the sunlit field. When one of them approached me, I realized it was a different sort of large animal and decided it was a wolf. (I knew about wolves because of the love my mother had for them.) This particular animal was so kind and gentle that I had absolutely no fear and was completely drawn to it. It felt to me like a soulmate type of energy, a protector. Wolves have, ever since, been the animal I feel most spiritually linked with.

The Waiting Station, as I understand it today, is our life in-between lives—an intermediate space between life and the afterlife where souls go to acclimate once again to being human while waiting to be birthed (or in my case, rebirthed) into a body. It's where we transition out of the spirit world. Here, we lose all the knowledge and freedom that we have in the spirit realm and simultaneously begin to relearn and adapt to the limiting rules of humanity.

As I relaxed in the grass, a brilliant light drew my attention to the top of a massive mountain to my left. The light, I realized, was another being, one I hadn't encountered before. I couldn't see who it was because it was so incredibly bright that it obscured every detail. The details didn't matter—the intensity of light seemed to be the point. And it was the most brilliant light I had ever laid eyes on. Thinking back, the intensity of it would probably blind a human—it was unlike anything I've ever seen on earth.

To this day, I cry whenever I talk about this powerful being of light. I didn't and still don't know who it was, but I knew they were all-knowing and more loving than any being I have ever encountered. I wanted so much to be as near to this loving essence as possible. I desperately wanted to climb the mountain to get to it, but I knew that I couldn't as it was too high and too steep. I wasn't meant to approach the being, only to see it, feel its power, and know it loved me unconditionally. I never saw this beautiful, brilliant light before, nor did I know what it represented at the time. Still, it *felt* like it was the keeper of all that was and always will be. This glowing being was utterly pure and safe and felt like the beauty of every living soul wrapped into one.

As this magnificent being continued to watch me from the mountaintop, I suddenly noticed other lights behind the trees in front of me. Though I couldn't make out exactly who they were, I knew they belonged to me and loved me very much. Then to my right, I noticed a lovely cottage made of stones. I could see rainbow colors in the stones, which felt like a refuge of such loving-kindness and peace. Once I noticed it, a new-to-me light angel seemed to float out of the cottage toward me. At that moment, I completely understood that it was my time to return to the body.

"It's time to go, Susie," the light angel confirmed as she drew closer.

As I stood to follow, everything faded into the background. She then took my hand, calmly walked me along a riverbank, and talked to me about my journey back home. She explained that water is the element that connects the spiritual with the material, and all souls come to earth through it.

"You're about to go through the water again. Are you ready?" she asked.

"I don't know. . . ." I replied, feeling confused.

"You're going back to be with your mommy," she explained further as we continued to walk next to the glistening, crystal-clear water. "You're going to go through many hardships in your life from this point forward. It's going to be very painful at times, but you will help many people. You're meant to be a healer, Susie; you're meant to help people heal their souls." The light angel paused for a moment for me to take it all in and then asked, "Do you understand? Are you willing to go now?"

"I'm still not sure. . . ." I was still feeling nervous.

Continuing down the riverbank, the light angel kept talking, telling me all about the life I was returning to and some things I would experience. She then told me that my mommy would be waiting for me when I returned, and never for a moment in this whole experience did I stop wanting her. Eventually, the nervousness dissipated, and I understood it was my job to be brave and return to my home.

Once I was ready to go, the light angel first let me see my mom on the earth plane. From my perspective in the spirit world, I couldn't read her mind, but I could see what she was doing (cleaning the house). I *felt* that soon I was going to be with her again and that I was going to be safe. The angel then taught me how to communicate with her telepathically—my first instruction in understanding spirit-to-human communication.

I began to say over and over to her, "Mommy, I'm in the freezer! Mommy, I'm in the freezer!"

This time, my mother heard it, in her words, "louder than a scream." This time she couldn't ignore it. I don't believe she thought it was coming from me; however, she dropped everything and ran to the garage to save her baby.

"It's time to step into the water now," the light angel said. She blew me a kiss, and I felt the gentle wind of her breath. The sun shone on my face, and there was bright-ness all around me as the light angel helped me into the river. It felt like a warm bath washing over my skin, like I was being purified in the water. As time passed, I came to embrace the warmth of understanding. Life might be difficult, but what I learned in the afterlife equipped my soul to bloom in the dark soil.

Seeing Spirits

When my mom opened the freezer, there I was with my back to her. She spun me around and found me ashen and lifeless. In her shock, she dropped me to run inside and call for help, and I fell to the garage floor and hit my chin, splitting it open. The impact of the fall brought me back to consciousness, and I took my first breath back.

When she returned, my mother sat on the floor, cried, and rocked me—and then she put me to bed. I wondered why she didn't take me to a hospital for a long time. Later in life, she told me this was because she feared that my alcoholic dad would get mad at her for what had happened to me that day. I was breathing and seemed fine, so she thought everything was okay. But when I woke up in the morning, she feared my brain may have had some slight damage, because I was suddenly seeing and hearing things that were so intense it was beyond her understanding and her own gifts from Spirit.

While I'd had mediumship experiences prior to this life-altering event, afterward I could see spirits literally *everywhere*—down the hallway, under my bed, in the corner of my room, outside the window—and it terrified me. Even though I remembered everything about my experience in the afterlife, I was still afraid. It is one thing to be surrounded by angels in the loving spiritual world, and another thing entirely being in the fear-based human world with different kinds of spirits constantly trying to get my attention. Though the spirits surrounding me were always very loving and kind, I was still a young child susceptible to the bogeyman.

Shortly after I returned, I remember standing at the edge of the doorway in my room, too scared to go to the potty because there were so many spirits down the hallway. Big groups of them were smiling at me and chattering unintelligibly to me. They were not trying to hurt me in any way, but my young self struggled to believe that, and adapting to this new reality was confusing. To make matters worse, I couldn't talk to my parents about it. I tried to of course, but learned very quickly that it was a big no-no.

Once, I woke up in the middle of the night and cried out in fear because spirits were surrounding my bed.

"What is it, Susie?" Mom asked, rushing into the room.

"Mommy, I'm afraid. These people are in my room, and they are scaring me."

"Who is in the room? I don't see them."

"The people are everywhere, talking to me and looking at me."

"Susie, listen to me: You never talk about the things that other people don't see. Okay? It's not safe to talk about those things. Nothing is here and no one is in the room."

I nodded my head and begged her to let me sleep with her. She wouldn't let me in the bed, but she put me on the floor next to her. Then when I turned toward the bed, I saw all the same spirits underneath! I quickly realized that there was nowhere to hide from my strange new reality. When I got too scared, they *did* leave me in peace, unless it was to relay something very important. I would sometimes even get sleep paralysis when the spirits needed to tell me something of significance. I couldn't move or blink, but I was fully conscious and heard everything they said. They would tell me their story, and I was as frozen as ice, so I had to listen. This eventually stopped much later in life when I stopped being fearful of their presence.

My support system as a young, sensitive intuitive wasn't strong, which resulted in me internalizing most everything. Looking back, I understand my mother's perspective. Sharing what she saw led her to be hospitalized and medicated. She didn't want to repeat that or for me to share that fate. My one saving grace was my sister, who also sensed the spirit world and has been my constant support system—from childhood to this day—because she understands it all firsthand. When I realized my mother would not help during my fearful episodes, I began to crawl into bed with my sister in the middle of the night.

"Sissy, I see things looking inside the window," I remember saying to her.

"I do too," she responded.

"You do?" I was surprised. "Who are they? I am scared."

"I don't know who they are, Susie, but I know they are not here to hurt us." She would always reassure me and make me feel safe during my formative years, and for that I was blessed.

The spirits became less scary as time passed and became my friends instead. There was a room in the house I grew up in where the spirits liked to congregate, and I would spend hours playing with them. I could see their reflection in the room's big bay window so clearly. My siblings called it the "creepy room," but I absolutely loved it. It made me feel like I had friends, someone to play with me and share in my loneliness. You see, I was obviously different from other children my age. I was a tender and kind little girl who wanted to be loved and give love. While kids were growing up and coming into their own, I was looking for love and acceptance, which doesn't always come easy with children. This continued throughout most of my childhood and partly into my adulthood.

Spirit and Vibration

Seeing as the spirits were my best friends after returning from my near-death experience, people often wonder if I ever asked them about the abuse—why it was happening, why weren't they protecting me, and could they make it stop? The answer to that is, no, I didn't, because the truth of the matter is that I did not know it was abnormal. Like I said, I simply was too little to understand.

Of course, as an adult who has worked hard to overcome this trauma, I have had some hard talks with Spirit! This is what I learned: Spirit doesn't *allow* these terrible things to happen; they happen because evil is in the minds of man. As much as our spirit teams want to help us in these kinds of terrible situations, they cannot interfere with our free will, including people with bad intentions. They can and do attempt to send us messages and warnings, but in general our vibrations are too low to perceive them. If we do perceive them, we tend to either ignore them or not understand them. Children's connection to the spirit world is still mostly intact, so they often hear messages but fail to fully understand them.

This is why I am passionate about relaying the importance of raising our vibrations while on this planet. By default, humans vibrate extremely low. Think of it as if we are energetic sloths—as lovable and capable and precious as sloths are, they are extremely slow-moving. The spirits, in contrast, are like hummingbirds. The sloth might sense a hummingbird nearby, but by the time it is able to turn its head and body to perceive it, the hummingbird has already been there and moved along to a million other places! In this analogy, a medium would be like a butterfly: we still miss a lot because the spirits are still vibrating much faster than us, but we are tuned in enough that we do pick some things up.

If we don't consciously work on raising our vibrations, we remain at a dense vibrational state, making it difficult for spirits to reach us. All they can do is hope that we hear them and make better choices. Rest, meditation, gratitude, music, laughing, dancing—anything that brings you true joy—will raise your vibration.

So, because of the relentless free will of humans, even to the point of choosing evil, Spirit and our spirit teams can't always protect us, despite wanting to. And it's meant to be that way because if we were protected from every single harm, what would we learn? How would our souls grow? There is a purpose to our negative and painful experiences, but I assure you our free will is involved. Spirits love us and want to help us. The question is: Are we listening?

Living in Two Worlds

Upon returning from my afterlife journey, I felt as if I were walking in two worlds at once. I always felt left out; I felt like I was constantly on the outside looking in, trying to figure out what other people were seeing and not seeing— what was "real" to everyone and what was my experience alone. I was always aware of the spirit world's unconditional love and acceptance, yet I was equally attached to being loved and accepted by my friends and family. This meant I was, ultimately, vibrating on two different levels of dimension. Without any control over it, unable to accurately discern what was "seen" and "unseen" by others, I was very confused during this time in my life, to say the least.

I was a child with the thought processes of a spiritually connected adult, resulting in a childhood of being teased and bullied. Not only was I extremely sensitive to the spirit world, but I was also highly empathic to the human world. I always tried to help people and animals and was acutely aware of everybody's emotions and feelings. I could feel other people's sadness, so I naturally became a little counselor, constantly asking people if they were okay and offering a listening ear. I was extremely hypersensitive to others' pain, and because of that, I *really* wanted to help people feel better. I felt in my soul that I was meant to help, but I had no idea how to harness my spiritual gifts at the time.

My neighborhood friends had no problem telling me that I was weird. One day, while playing in "the creepy room" with some neighborhood girls, I saw one of their grandmothers standing next to her.

"Your grandma is here, and she wants to play!" I told them, excitedly.

But the girls accused me of being mean because the girl's grandmother had very recently died.

"I know; she is really here and loves you and wants to play with us!" I tried to explain.

They laughed at and rejected me.

When I told my mom about the incident, she said, "I told you not to talk about it. . . ." And experiences like this indeed made me stay increasingly quiet and keep the spirit world to myself.

Another incident happened when I was around seven years old. My mom had a friend named Dottie who was dying, and my siblings were friends with Dottie's daughter, so one day we all went over to play. My mom instructed my older siblings not to allow me to see Dottie while we were there because she was just days away from passing. But when we arrived, I only wanted to sit with Dottie. My siblings disobeyed my mother, happy I was being kept busy so they could play.

"Why are you in this room, Susie?" Dottie asked me when I entered.

"I'm gonna sit here with you; I'm not scared," I said. "You're going to be okay. You're going to leave really soon, and you're not gonna have pain anymore."

"I know; I'm really excited for that to happen," she replied. "I've already seen the other side, and I'm ready to be there now."

"Isn't it so pretty there?"

"Yes, it is magnificent!"

I ended up spending the entire day sitting next to Dottie's bedside. In my child mind, she felt like a witch with pale, yellow-green skin, yet I was not afraid in the slightest. There was nowhere I'd rather be. Dottie and I chatted all day like this, and I told her everything I knew about the afterlife and how peaceful it was. At the end of our visit, I told her I loved her. I never saw her alive again. It wasn't until I came home that afternoon and told my mother what had happened that she informed me that Dottie had not been consciously aware throughout our whole conversation.

I have endless stories of being treated differently because of my spiritual abilities when I was young. If I'm honest, I didn't much like being on this planet for a long time on my journey because it was so confusing and painful. I was only half here, and I didn't know how to control or harness the other spirit-connected half yet. But, again, our darkest hours pave golden paths for us, and today I have so many mothers bringing their children to me who don't feel they fit in and are sometimes bullied relentlessly. I'm a medium—why are they bringing bullied kids to me? Because Spirit knows I've experienced it and I've healed, so I'm most often able to help these children overcome their traumas too.

As a child, the cruelty I received when sharing about the spirit world with others made me bury my gift publicly until the day came, much later, that I chose to develop as a medium. But privately, I never stopped living in both worlds. When I was in my early 20s, my sister-in-law, Erin, who was also one of my friends, developed a malignant brain tumor and was preparing her soul to cross. I was worried that she would cross over before I had an opportunity to say good-bye once more. When I called the hospital to check on her, as I always did throughout the day, they said that everything was fine and all her stats were up. Yet, soon after I hung up, I was sitting at my computer working when I felt a massive rush of energy go through my body, starting at the tips of my toes all the way up through my crown. I could actually *feel* Erin like she was moving inside of me. I felt her soul pass *through* my body, into my soul, out the top of my head, and simultaneously as that was happening, I heard her whisper, *Thank you, I love you, good-bye.*

I began sobbing because I knew at that moment, despite what the hospital had just said, Erin was gone. I have never felt a soul enter into my body so strongly, and to this day, it was one of the most profound experiences I have ever had. Fifteen minutes later, my dad called me upstairs.

"Erin died. . . ." I said when I walked into the room.

"Erin died," he repeated.

Living in My Abnormally Normal Reality

My new way of life was to walk among the "dead."
You'll notice that the word *dead* here and in this chapter's
title is in quotations. That's because this word isn't really
correct. Dead means "no longer alive," and while it's true
that our physical bodies become lifeless upon death, our
spiritual souls are very much flourishing. The word *dead*
suggests nonexistence, but our existence, in truth, is eternal. We don't really die; we merely return to our spiritual
home to continue genuinely living. Whenever they do
return to our collective spiritual home, the "dead" among
us still have things to say, still want to contribute, and still
want to be a dynamic part of our lives—they want us to
keep them alive in our heads and hearts. And when we
die, we, too, will want to relay our aliveness to our loved
ones still on earth; we will want to be kept alive inside of
them. The truth is our soul's greatest calling is to be as
alive as possible.

Living life among the living dead was a double-edged
sword—it could be so beautiful and profound, but it could
also be so painfully confusing and lonely. I felt so different, yet I didn't know what that difference was. Imagine being a fish out of water, flopping on land, and then
suddenly someone throws water on you, and for a while,
you're no longer flopping—you're back in your element,
yet not entirely. That's how it felt upon returning from my
afterlife experience and for most of my life after that.

In this analogy, I knew my true home was the water
(spirit world), yet I was momentarily living on land (material world), with water constantly being splashed onto
me, keeping me spiritually alive. In a world where most
thought the material world was our true home, not only
did I learn that we are actually of the water while I was on

the other side, but also my new reality from this point on was to be reminded of it every single day. This was what living among the "dead" felt like to me.

Walking in two worlds occurred throughout my life, but for so long, I didn't understand it—it *just was*. Adjusting back to "normal" with my "abnormal" gift was one of my life's big trials, but as time went on, I got used to living in my "abnormally normal" reality, as I've come to call it.

Years later, after returning from my afterlife experience and accepting this ability as a regular synergy between spirits and myself, every day has been full of amazing interactions with them. I've been at restaurants and watched someone's deceased mother sitting across the table, trying to get their attention, unbeknownst to anyone but me. I've been awakened in the middle of the night to spirits telling me so-and-so died, and they have a message to relay to someone. I've been to funerals and have seen the person being honored there, literally, in spirit, watching over their service and turning to me to say, "Isn't this so beautiful?!"

I'd always wondered what was "wrong" with me, I knew I was different, but I did *not* know I was a medium—I didn't even know what that was! It wasn't until much later, when James Van Praagh and Lisa Williams, among others, shared with me that I was a "true medium." Then and only then was I able to take the leap of faith required to answer my calling.

INTEGRATION MOMENT
Keeping the "Dead" Alive

In this chapter, we learned that our deceased loved ones are always all around us, whether we can sense it or not. Much like electricity, just because we can't see it with our eyes does not mean it isn't there for us to tap into at all times. We also learned that our loved ones want to be kept alive in our heads and hearts. Choose any of the following prompts to dive into your relationship with the spirit world:

- Water is the connecting element between the spiritual and material worlds. What is your relationship like with water? How could you bring more of it into your life to bring more spiritual energy to your material world?

- Being bullied as a child has allowed me to help children who are bullied today. What is something in your life that you overcame that you could now use to help others?

- Our deceased loved ones want to stay alive in our heads and hearts. How have you kept your "dead" alive?

- In what ways have spirits tried communicating with you, even if you wrote it off as nonsense at the time?

- Throughout your life, have you ever felt like you were on the outside looking in and didn't fit in?

Chapter Exercises

Our loved ones enjoy communicating with us in different ways. Keeping our deceased loved ones alive in our thoughts can bring us emotional pain, but it does help us to create a connection beyond the veil. The hard part is to *trust* and *believe* that they are there walking among us. They, too, have a veil and are not able to read our minds or see private things. Your intention must be set for them to hear you in order for them to do so. (I do, however, see them joining in the holiday festivities whenever they have the opportunity.)

Let's practice some ways in which we can acknowledge our deceased loved ones and connect with them:

- Read books about the afterlife. This will help you achieve a deeper understanding that death is simply a transition into a different dimension, not the final end.

- List the ways in which you have continued to have a relationship with your loved ones by speaking to them and engaging with them in your life. Even if only to say good morning and goodnight.

- In what ways do you give your loved ones ample time and opportunities to visit? Are you open to receiving messages?

- Prepare a meeting time and a safe space to connect. Let your loved ones in spirit know you're open to them. Try to meet in the same spot each and every time you set a date to be with them. For me, that is late at night while I am in bed and at my office, where I do my readings.

- Allow the words you are sensing to go from hand to paper. Write what they are channeling through you. Don't think; write.

- During your dinner, have a conversation with them and see what comes into your head. Conversing with them helps them to feel the connection also.

- If you sense they are around, acknowledge them. In what ways have you felt their presence in your day?

- Bring them with you when you are soaking in the tub, showering, or simply strolling along the coast. They love water; it is a clear and defining spiritual connection for all involved. Spirits work with high-vibrational energy. Raising your vibration can be as simple as thinking of all your joyful times together, listening to music, and dancing. Don't allow fear to stop you from connecting. Your loved ones are waiting to speak to you.

- The most powerful way they speak to you is in dreams. This is a peaceful experience where every moment of the visitation is clear and feels so real that you know they are there with you. They often do this to show you they are okay and that they love you. (You'll learn more about dream visitations in Chapter 8.) You can ask a loved one to enter into your dreams right before you head off to sleep. Tell them this is your heart's desire. They are listening and will do their best. Be patient—it takes them time to figure out that energetic process.

CHAPTER 6

Becoming a Medium

My decades of firsthand experience with the spirit world have taught me that, whether we are aware of it or not, we *all* walk among spirits—every single one of us, no exceptions. This is because we *are* Spirit, and sensing a connection with the unseen spirit world is merely a matter of whether we are plugged in or not. Think of a lamp: If it isn't plugged into an electrical socket, it doesn't light up—but does that mean electricity doesn't exist? Applying this analogy to a spiritual lens, Spirit is the electricity and humans are the lamps. We can all connect with the spirit world; we must choose (free will!) to plug in.

Eventually, my life's purpose was revealed to me that I should serve as a spiritual medium, which is someone who is able to see the unseen world and provide "spiritual enlightenment," so to speak, connecting humanity to the spirit world. Still, the path wasn't an overnight thing. It took a lot of time, detours, and convincing for me to feel confident enough to do mediumship professionally. (And, trust me, confidence in this line of work is something I still work on every day!) I rejected my gift of spirit communication throughout my adolescent and teen years. I was more concerned with trying to fit into the "real" world, which meant I needed to escape the spirit world by any means necessary. While I could quiet the noise, I found I could never *fully* disconnect. I was still having persistent dreams and visitations and spending a lot of time trying to understand what was happening to me.

It wasn't until my late teens, when my nana died, that I began to take these spirit visitations more seriously. I was extremely close to my nana, and her death was the first significant loss in my life. Her spirit came to me one night before I knew she was gone, when I was lying in bed but still very awake.

"I was alone for so many years, and nobody visited me," I heard someone say. I looked up at the foot of my bed and saw a person I didn't immediately recognize, sitting in what I sensed was a rocking chair.

"Go away, go away!" I chanted. I had been doing that for years to quiet the perpetual spirits. But soon enough, my soul recognized her familiar manner. "Nana," I asked, "is it you?"

"Yes, I am here to say good-bye," she replied. "You're going to find out tomorrow morning that I left your world, but *we don't die*, Susie! I want you to know that I'm still here. I'm happy and healthy. I am no longer alone, and I love you."

I remember lying there thinking, *This truly was real.* I had never had someone that close to me visit me from the spirit world, and I could *feel her* so clearly. She felt so light and happy—so free. It was no surprise to learn the next day that my nana had passed the night before, at the very time she had visited me.

After this visit, I felt more confused and alone than ever. I had spent so many years trying to quiet that side of myself, convincing myself I was just weird. This visit from my nana meant I could no longer deny how real it all was, and it scared me. Still, I decided to stop avoiding my "experiences" and finally look deeper into them—which wasn't a simple Google search in those days! I had to find a parapsychology center, then work up the nerve to call them. A kind man answered, who I proceeded to open up to. I shared what had been happening to me for so long.

"I see," he replied after I finished. "Well, it sounds to me like you're a medium talking with the spirit world."

"What's *that*?"

"It's a person who can talk to the dead."

Whaaaaaat?! I remember thinking. I had no idea what he was talking about, and it both scared and excited me. I hung up the phone and didn't tell a soul.

Keeping My Secret

After my revelation via the kind man at the parapsychology center, I began reading about mediumship. I mostly kept my secret to myself, but sometimes things would slip out in a public way.

"Oh, you're pregnant!" I said to my neighbor one day.

"No, no," she responded. "I'm preparing for the in vitro next week, though."

"No—you're pregnant now with a little girl." I couldn't help saying it. I *knew* it was true because Spirit was there telling me. She looked at me like I was out of my mind, but three days later, she told me she was pregnant. And then she never spoke to me again. Over time, I realized it was best to keep my experiences with the spirit world to myself.

My path eventually led me to working as a grief and addiction counselor. It felt like a natural calling, as my life's purpose was to help others. Unbeknownst to my clients, I could hear, see, and feel the presence of their departed loved ones and felt their energy coming from the spirit world. Even though I wasn't yet embracing my mediumship abilities, I started sharing with my clients the messages I was receiving from souls on the other side. However, I kept the true source of the insight private. My clients began referring their grieving friends to the "special" addiction counselor. This marked the beginning of my gradual shift from grief and addiction counseling to mediumship. Consequently, I began offering voluntary mediumship readings at grief groups and hospices.

Even as I consciously utilized my gift, I still struggled to trust it fully. What ultimately convinced me that my gift was trustworthy was an experience one evening on a crowded shuttle with my friends in Las Vegas. As we came to an abrupt stop, I accidentally fell back and touched another passenger's knee. *Oh my God*, I thought, *his life energy feels unusually low.* Spirit then relayed to me that this gentleman may be leaving the planet very soon. But when I told my friends, they were irritated. "We're in Vegas, where we're supposed to be having fun. Why would you talk about something like that?"

"Lighten up, Susan!" was definitely the theme of my growing up and early adult years.

On another occasion, I was at a party where people started openly discussing a high-profile missing child case in the news. Suddenly, I saw the whole story of how the child was taken by her uncle. I began to tell my friends what I saw, but again, everyone reminded me we were at a party, and I should stop being so somber. Of course, later, the story of the missing child was solved, and I learned Spirit had given me the correct information.

Time passed, and I decided to take a course with a famous medium, James Van Praagh. He called me out from the crowd at the event and asked me to stand up. When I did, he asked if the information he brought through on stage made sense to me.

"Yes, what you are saying makes sense to me," I replied.

"You have natural mediumship abilities; you've had a near-death experience," he said.

"Yes, I have," I replied.

"You see spirits all the time, don't you?"

"Maybe . . ." I felt shy, put on the spot, and afraid of what others might think.

"Be honest," he said, "because this is something you need to be doing—you *will* do this in the future to help others heal their grief. I hope you start soon."

One day, many years later, I finally felt ready to understand on a deeper level, so I attended an event by the medium Lisa Williams. Hundreds of people were there, and in the middle of the event, Lisa called me up to the venue's center aisle. When I approached, she discussed my near-death experience with as much detail as if she had been there with me. I had no idea what was happening.

Lisa spoke to the audience after the lights were turned on me. She said, "There are spirits everywhere around her." Then she looked at me and explained that my near-death experience had created strong abilities in me and that I belonged on stage like her.

I was taken aback by her words and denied them firmly. I was still skeptical of my capabilities.

"Yes, you belong on a stage like me," she insisted. "In fact, your father and your brothers are here in spirit, and they want you to know that they will help you on this journey; you just need to take a leap of faith. This is not a 'you *should* do this work' situation—it's a 'you *must*.'"

Lisa continued to read me accurately and precisely, and I was utterly mesmerized by her. When I eventually saw some of the photos people took that day, there were orbs of light everywhere around me, so bright that I was hardly visible.

It had become difficult to deny the consensus, what James, Lisa, and many of my teachers said: I was a true medium. So, I decided to do as my family on the other side had instructed—I took a leap of faith.

Embracing My Mediumship Abilities

Luckily my family *here*, on this side, was also extremely supportive of my decision to jump full force into professional mediumship—yes, including my teenage children and my otherwise level-headed husband! They were used to me doing mediumship non-professionally by this point, so it wasn't a stretch for them. For me, taking this leap of faith meant learning to accept myself, who I am, and what I am here to do. And that meant I had to look at it, at me, head-on—it meant I had to heal.

I spent the next several years taking mediumship courses to better understand and further develop my abilities. I wanted to learn *how* I knew things. At my core, I am an intellectual, so I studied, studied, studied. I took numerous courses with Lisa and James, among other notable teachers of the time. I began to learn so much—not only about the magical inner workings of mediumship but, most importantly, about *me*. About *who I am*.

I began with a basic class in turning the messages on and off so that I could control the spirit messages coming through at all hours. Finally, I could sleep at night in silence! I then took advanced mediumship courses which consisted of practicing and trusting the messages that came through. Thinking back on the lost child I might've helped years ago, I also took forensic mediumship courses to learn techniques to help locate the missing.

I then had the privilege of studying under the esteemed Dr. Raymond Moody, a psychiatrist and writer who coined the term "near-death experience" in his research. I received my doctorate of divinity from the School of Mystical Arts where Dr. Moody taught. I had always admired him, sensing he would understand me on a different level than a layperson. He was everything I thought he would be and more.

A brilliant teacher and a good, kind man, Raymond Moody taught me the philosophical background and impact of my gift. He taught me that these gifts, among others, have been around since the beginning of time and that all we had to do was learn about philosophy to understand this truth. I will forever be grateful for my time with him.

Born This Way

It's essential for me to convey that mediumship is not an extension of me; it *is* me and always has been. It's not something I wished to bring into my life; it *is* my life and an innate part of my soul. Over the years, many people have minimized my abilities as weird, woo-woo, or even downright evil. "You're doing the devil's work!" I've heard this more times than you can imagine. This profoundly hurts me because these kinds of sentiments insult my soul's essence. In actuality, it is not what I am but *who I am*. To judge or attack someone based on who they are is fundamentally unjust, and that is how these judgments feel to me. We all know about the infamous "witch trials." Though we aren't burning people at the stake in today's world, it's still a battle for people like me to be accepted for who we are—not who we "chose" to be, *who we are*.

Granted, things are much better today than ever before for people who work with the spirit world. This allows spiritual healers of all kinds to become more and more authentically themselves. Authenticity—not hiding any part of ourselves—is such an important lesson for us *all* to learn while incarnated into human bodies. The Creator created every single one of us to be exactly who we are, not to live in shame by hiding select parts of ourselves. When we bury pieces of ourselves, that's when darkness enters.

Evil is in the minds of men. Spirit isn't evil, but human consciousness can be, and being unauthentic is a pathway to calling that in. Spirit created us all purposely unique. Our mission while having this human experience is to dare to be our true selves.

Spirit created me this way, and I now accept that I was born to serve humanity through mediumship work. I studied and practiced intensely to do what I do *correctly*— but not perfectly. I strengthened the spiritual muscle that being a medium requires and mastered the ethics necessary to handle the sensitive parts of people's lives, but the innate gift was always there from day one.

Every single one of us has a natural divine gift. Whether it's a creative gift such as writing, painting, or music; an inherent mastery of science, medicine, or business; or any number of roles of service in between, there is something that comes naturally to us all that we are meant to tap into in our lifetime. In fact, these gifts and passions are so important to us that most of us define ourselves by them: "I am a writer," "I am a doctor," "I am a teacher." For me, the gift is the ability to see the unseen, make sense of the senseless, and comfort those in suffering by reminding them of their eternal connection to Spirit. I am a medium.

Being a medium doesn't ensure a constant ability to connect with someone's energy during a reading. There are times when the energy isn't aligned or ready, and it's crucial to recognize that professional expertise in any field doesn't equate to absolute perfection. Remember that being a medium can be a very painful and challenging field, as we are attempting to hold space for our clients' deepest wounds and trying to help them with the intensive healing process of grief.

This chapter is titled "Becoming a Medium," but the truth is that I didn't *become* a medium; I was *born* one and have always been one. It was my soul's contract to do this work. The *real* journey was understanding, eventually accepting, and trusting that truth. The real journey for you, for me, for all of us, is self-love, which begins with self-acceptance. In the last chapter, I discussed how living in two worlds at once left me feeling like a fish out of water, but don't we *all* feel like a fish out of water in this human existence? Don't we all feel like we're different and alone? Don't we all feel, at times, rejected and dejected during our life journey? Don't we all feel like we're not enough? And don't we all crave love and acceptance? The goal in every individual's journey is to foster deep self-acceptance and self-love. This is our truest soul purpose, and this is what the journey of "becoming a medium" has meant for me.

For clarity, I'd like to note here that a soul purpose is the broader, spiritual mission of an individual across lifetimes, which I believe for all of us is the acceptance of self and self-love. Each person's life purpose, on the other hand, is specific to each soul's goals and contributions in their current earthly existence. My life purpose is to be a healer, which led to my stepping into my role as a professional medium.

That said, even once I committed to my studies of mediumship development, it took me a very long time to adopt the word *medium*. For so much of my life, I was terrified of being rejected for seeing spirits, fearful of being locked up like my mother was for a psychotic break, being found schizophrenic like my brother, or simply someone, *anyone*, thinking in their hearts that I was evil. As a lifelong people pleaser, I cared *a lot* about what others thought of me, so not until about 18 years ago did I really have enough confidence to accept the title "medium" fully—to accept *me* fully.

If I had to pinpoint the moment when I finally accepted that I was a medium, it was when I was participating in a development group with nearly 30 other students. I started to read someone, and then something came over me, and I couldn't stop; I read most everyone in the room! I went from one person to the next to the next, and everything flowed through me. It was a feeling I'd never felt because, at that moment, souls on the other side were talking through me; finally, *I knew it*. My journey of talking to spirits has been riddled with insecurity, fear, and reluctance to trust. I always questioned myself—as I said, I was always my biggest skeptic. But this was the first time I was certain: It wasn't insanity. It was spirits.

Afterward, the group instructor said, "Susan, you are a *really gifted* medium, and you will help many with your abilities."

From there, I had to stop hiding who I was and "come out of the closet" as a medium, and it was the most overwhelming thing I've ever done. I'll never forget writing to my friends and family on Facebook: "I'm a medium; I talk to spirits. I will understand if you are uncomfortable with that fact and choose not to remain my friend." I published the post and began sobbing tears of relief immediately after. It was the first time in my life that I could really breathe because I wasn't hiding anymore. Finally, I felt free.

Lessons Learned through Mediumship

I truly understand how difficult it is for people to trust what they can't see. But as I learned on the Yellow Brick Road, we are meant to do just that: to develop faith in that which we cannot see, in spirits, allowing the golden path they have paved for us to unfold. Using the lamp analogy once again, we may not fully grasp the understanding of electricity, yet we still plug in our lamps to enjoy the illumination they provide. Similarly, even if we cannot perceive the invisible realm of spiritual energy, it doesn't imply that it doesn't exist or that we can't reap its rewards. By tapping into this unseen dimension, we can enrich our lives and enhance our well-being.

We each have the ability to connect personally with our angels, guides, and loved ones in spirit. No, that doesn't mean that everyone's purpose is to pursue mediumship professionally. We all have divine gifts specific to us that our souls choose prior to incarnating here that will help us grow the way we most need. But we can all connect personally with our spirit teams, and doing so helps us as we learn to trust our unique divine paths.

Professional mediums serve as bridges to the spiritual realm. Our heartfelt mission is to help you personally connect with it, allowing you to experience truth—love transcends death. Because, as my nana said, and Spirit has repeatedly confirmed, we don't die.

But if we don't die, what becomes of us, exactly? This is the question I spend most of my days trying to help people understand. Anyone who has ever lost someone close to them is deeply concerned about what happened to their loved one—where did they go, if anywhere, and are they okay?

Although our physical bodies wither when we die, our consciousness does not. We take our consciousness with us because it is a part of our soul. Soul growth comes by way of healing the conscious things we did or didn't do in our cumulative lifetimes.

We are here on earth to do this soul work firsthand, but it's a misconception that the work stops on the other side. We are meant to expand ourselves and refine our consciousness, both in our human and spiritual states of being. *As above, so below.* Our conscious choices are *the pathway* to soul growth.

That's why I've committed to "cleaning up my side of the street," to correct and purify my thoughts and deeds at every opportunity. This means taking responsibility for my own actions, resolving personal issues, or making amends in order to improve my behavior or situation, without focusing on others' faults or problems. It's about being accountable for my own actions and behaviors to promote healing and personal growth. I encourage everyone I work with to "clean up their side of the street" as well. I don't always consummately achieve this higher calling; however, it is imperative that we learn to do this, and for me personally, my work depends on it.

I can always tell when I am muddied in my own consciousness because my connection to the spirit world is muddied, and it's more difficult for me to do my work well. But the minute I spend time cleaning up my side of the street, everything feels clear, and my link with Spirit again becomes solid. But whether one works professionally as a medium or not, this is a crucial component for everyone to understand: the cleaner our mind, the more connected to Spirit we become. I encourage you, in whatever situation that is creating grief in you, to do your best to take an honest look at your personal responsibility, make amends, and then forgive yourself for your part.

People often say that time heals all wounds. Although this is a comforting saying, it's truly *how* we utilize our time that brings about healing. In our pursuit to cleanse our consciousness in the afterlife, we should prioritize refining our thoughts and actions while we're still on earth. As individuals approach the end of their lives, the urgency to make amends grows stronger. As we embark on the journey of transition, we come to realize that our thoughts and deeds in this world will accompany us into the next. It's in everyone's best interest to strive for resolution and inner peace as much as possible. And that is what true healing is—a process of looking at ourselves, not pointing the finger elsewhere.

This is what is addressed in "shadow work," which involves looking at the things you've long been hiding inside of yourself, the things that are hard to look at and you'd rather not deal with. The haunting things that follow you like a shadow. And that is how it happened with me as well—I got to a place in my life where I *had* to look at the shadowy parts of myself that I had buried away in self-preservation, or else. This included working through the big traumas of my life: the sexual abuse, the grief of my many family suicides, and my inability to have biological children. By working with a shaman that specialized in shadow work I was able to learn how to help myself self-heal and recognize the value of all that I have been through, even, and especially, the dark parts.

That very same healing is what, ultimately, took me from having mediumship qualities to being a working medium. If I hadn't looked honestly at myself and healed the trauma that had stacked up in my life, I could not do this work professionally. The moment I embraced the energy of healing, my life's purpose began to unfold before me like a golden pathway. As I continued to heal and foster more healing, the path broadened even further. This transformative experience holds true for each and every one of us.

INTEGRATION MOMENT
How Do You See the Unseen?

There is so much more to us than just our thinking. Getting in touch with our intuition and authenticity is key when developing our connection with the unseen world of spirit. Just because someone isn't a professional medium doesn't mean they can't have their own deep relationship with their loved ones and guides in the spirit world. Use the following questions to explore your relationship with the unseen and how you might deepen it:

- What was your perception of mediumship or a medium when you were growing up? Where did that perception come from? What are your thoughts now?

- Have you ever seen the "unseen?" If yes, have you ever talked about it with anyone? What happened, and how did it affect your life journey?

- What are your unique divine gifts, and what do they mean to you? Is there something that you've always wanted to do that you felt gifted in and passionate about but were pressured to do something different? What would it take for you to explore it now?

- What parts of yourself are you hiding that prevent you from being fully authentic? What would it take for you to take a leap of faith?

- In what ways have you "cleaned up your side of the street" already in your life? What outstanding issues are muddying your consciousness now that you might begin to face?

Chapter Exercises

Spirits are around us all the time, whether knowingly or unknowingly. Have you ever felt a strange sensation, or a shadow go past you, and no one was there when you turned to see who it was? When you learn how to tap into your abilities to feel and sense the spirit world, you can recognize when your loved ones or other spirits are there.

You don't have to become a professional medium. Everyone has abilities! You were born with the capability to tap into the five senses. These five senses are like muscles; when exercised, these muscles open the pathway. The sixth sense is our intuition, which can become stronger with practice and willingness. When you work to harness your own intuitive gifts, the world, seen and unseen, becomes a much larger, brighter, and more exciting place to be.

Here we will explore a few exercises that can help open up the pathways that connect you to the spirit world:

- You begin building your psychic senses by practicing. Try guessing what someone is going to say or the next song that's going to play. Ask yourself who is calling before looking at your phone. These are excellent intuition practice exercises.

- Think of times when you "just knew" something and it came to fruition. Write those instances down. It will help you begin the trust process necessary to experience mediumship. There is an inner voice inside of you. Honor it! The information they send goes through you as a whisper most times, if you can trust that soft inner voice!

- Find a place you can go that feels safe. Call in your loved ones without expectation.

- Try relaxing your mind while remaining in your body. It takes practice. You can be the conduit when you allow your mind to rest in meditation or with breathing techniques. Remember to stay in your body—the more grounded you are, the better the connection. Have you ever driven from A to Z and don't remember driving to your destination? Yet you got there safely. That is what relaxing the mind feels like.

- Work on letting go of your limiting beliefs through positive affirmations. (See the exercise in Chapter 1.) Tell yourself "all things are possible" many times a day. Some studies say doing this for 26 days can begin the process of changing your brain's pattern of disbelief. By day 63, you will have let go of your limiting beliefs.

- Write down your reactions when you sense something is there and feels different in the room. Watch for physical responses like butterflies or goosebumps; maybe your hair stands on end. These responses are higher vibrational responses to spirits.

- Join an intuition development group in your area taught by a skilled medium.

These are just a few ways to begin to understand mediumship and how to connect with your loved ones. Does this mean you will become a professional medium? Maybe not, but to speak with your loved ones on the other side, you must be willing to begin. Please remember this will not happen overnight—it's a marathon, not a sprint.

CHAPTER 7

Visitations

Every grief story is a love story. When we lose someone we love, we grieve. The deeper we have loved, the more we will grieve the loss. No one is immune to it—it is the one grand leveler. One of the greatest lessons of my life has been to realize that we don't decide when we are done with grief; the intensity of grief decides when it's done with us. In our fast-paced, instant-gratification culture, grief is one of the most painful lessons and certainly takes its time. Yet my decades of professional work with grief, both as a counselor and a medium, have shown me that one thing above all others expedites the bereavement healing process: the firsthand understanding that death does not *end* a relationship; it *changes* a relationship.

Death is not a final good-bye—it's a *bon voyage*. Grief, then, is the pain of *temporary* separation. It's a very real, deep, and often unbearable pain, but it's *not* forever. We will all return home to each other, and in the meantime, we still have the ability to communicate with our loved ones who have passed. And it's when we understand through direct, evidence-based communication with the afterlife that a relationship with our loved one remains that we can genuinely begin the healing journey.

The Windbridge Research Center studies "dying, death, and what comes next," and their current research confirms that "grief is resolved when the bereaved are able to recognize their continuing bonds with the deceased," and that "ADCs [After-Death Communications] have been demonstrated to dramatically reduce grief."* It's wonderful that society has come so far that we are now able to scientifically study taboo topics such as death and the afterlife, but this is something I've known for decades to be true, regardless of the science, because I see it every single day in my office.

In this chapter, I will showcase the remarkable healing potential of spiritual communication by sharing a selection of profoundly impactful client experiences. Selecting the most compelling examples was quite challenging, given the abundance of powerful stories I have encountered. Though it was a long, winding journey to understand and accept myself as a medium, today I can confidently say what the angels shared with me as a child about what would come of my life and how I would serve Spirit has absolutely come true. The comfort and healing my clients receive from connecting with their loved ones are why I've developed and maintained the courage to do this work.

Evidential Healing

Evidential mediums, which is what I am, communicate with your loved ones in spirit and bring back information as *evidence* that they still exist and are in your

---

*"Grief and After-death Communication," Windbridge Research Center, https://www.windbridge.org/grief-and-adc.

life. This evidence should be specific and clear so you can identify who is coming through. Recognizing your loved ones' continued existence and hearing their messages can be incredibly healing.

One of the most memorable readings I've had involved a father who had lost his daughter to an illness. He came into my office a complete skeptic, arms crossed and lips pursed. Reading his body language, I asked the spirits for as much evidence as they could give me during this particular session. When his daughter came through, she was extremely detailed, knowing her dad would need that.

"Your daughter is here, and she's telling me that she passed from a brain tumor."

He confirmed this, clearly shocked.

"She's telling me you used to play baseball together; it was one of her favorite memories with you."

"Oh my God, yes, yes we did that all the time," he said, slowly uncrossing his arms. His face began to relax.

"And she says you were at the lake together just before she passed, about a month before, and that you had to rescue her when she fell in."

When I shared her pet name for him, tears began streaming down his cheeks. "She really is here, isn't she? I came to you not believing, and I'm leaving a believer. I feel like I can now survive my grief." At the end of the reading, he jumped up and hugged me, crying on my shoulder.

These are precisely the kind of moments that make my job remarkable. Interactions with skeptics are not an unusual part of my job. I frequently remind individuals that my purpose is not to persuade them of my mediumship abilities but rather to encourage them to broaden their perspectives on the realm of possibilities.

❀ ❀ ❀

Sometimes I need to ask spirits to send a lot of very specific evidence in order to get their messages across to their very skeptical family. This happened once at a group mediumship reading, when the spirit of a father came to me.

"I am hearing the name William," I said, addressing the room. "I am being told his son Daniel is here with his family? He says he died from a heart attack called a widow maker and that he is a mechanic by trade, but also loved to bake. Does this make sense to anyone?"

"That sounds like it could be my grandfather," a young woman replied with trepidation. "My father is his son, Daniel, and he's sitting there," she said, pointing. "We are all family in this row."

William's spirit then proceeded to show me a motorcycle and camping. I heard the word "Sequoia." I relayed the information exactly as it came through to me.

"Yes, oh my God, yes, that's him!" the woman said through tears, looking at her father Daniel for confirmation. I could tell he was the true skeptic of the bunch.

I then asked the whole family to please stand up as I continued delivering the information the soul wanted to share.

"Daniel, your father's telling me that he is with your mother, your grandmother, your brother, and your grandfather. I'm also hearing that your name and your son's name are the same."

Daniel remained quiet but was visibly taken aback.

"Did your father teach you to bake?" I went on. "Because your father is showing me with pride you teaching your own son how to bake."

"Yes, yes, yes." Surprise filling his voice, Daniel finally broke his silence. "But that could apply to anyone, right?"

I told Daniel's father and other relatives in the spirit world that their family on earth needed more concrete evidence before they'd truly believe. William then proceeded to give me some very direct, personal information.

"Daniel, your father is now telling me that he was there in the room in spirit hours before and during the time your grandfather left the planet. He helped your grandfather to cross over. He is also sharing that you have a child who is autistic that isn't here with us right now."

Daniel began to choke up. "Everything you're saying is accurate."

I then turned to the Daniel's daughter. "Your grandmother said you are looking for one of her recipes. She didn't like to bake like your grandfather did; this recipe is for a dinner she made every year, and someone recently was asking for it. It's a very special recipe. I believe it's what she is known for."

"Yes," she confirmed excitedly. "My sister and I were discussing that recipe on the way here. We said we hope Grandma comes through to let us know where to find it!"

"Well, she is telling me it fell behind the stove. Look there and you will find it." (When they returned home, they texted me to confirm they found it in that exact spot!)

At this point, tears were flowing onstage and out in the audience, including Daniel and his entire family. Still, I could see that even with all the evidence, Daniel wasn't totally convinced that his family members in spirit were actually present. Something continued to hold him back.

Spending too much time on one reading while in a group setting is unfair to the rest of the audience, so I knew I had to move on soon—or so I thought. As I turned to finish with that particular family, something more came to me from Daniel's father: "My son has four strips of paper in his wallet, and they all contain important birth and death dates of our family."

I stopped in my tracks, turned around, and asked Daniel to stand up again.

"I just want to tell you one last thing. Your father's saying that you have four separate strips of paper in your wallet, on which you have written special family dates. Do you understand that?"

Daniel immediately started to cry. "How could you know that?" he asked. "Oh my God, he's really here!" Then he told the whole group that he carried the strips of paper in his wallet as a tribute to his many departed family members. The papers had the anniversary dates of his loved ones; therefore, they had special meaning to him.

❀ ❀ ❀

The heartbreaking loss of a child needs deep healing, and evidential mediumship can be the catalyst for that. When a mother and father came into my office one day, I could immediately sense their great pain, even though they said nothing. As the reading went on, I felt the powerful presence of a child and heard the name Tina over and over.

"In the room with me is a little girl in spirit whose heart was not strong enough to keep her here on the planet. Who is Tina?"

Staring at me in complete shock, the woman glanced at her husband before replying for them both. "Tina is our three-year-old daughter who recently passed away from a heart issue."

As the reading went further, I said to the couple, "Tina wants you to know that she is safe and with her Oma and Opa, and they are taking good care of her."

Tina's parents exclaimed, "This is what we came to hear. This is what we needed to know in order to heal this terrible loss." They held each other and cried tears of pain and joy. This evidence opened up the door to discussing their grief in depth, resulting in a beautiful breakthrough moment of healing.

When a reading brings forth such profound results, the client wonders, *How did she know that?!* But *I* am also thinking, *How did I know that?!* It's so miraculous to watch spiritual healing begin, especially in such a heart-wrenching situation as losing a child.

❀ ❀ ❀

Sometimes, people who have passed visit me *before* a reading. It's always a surprise to me! One morning, this happened while I was in the shower. At first, I panicked because . . . well, I was naked in the shower! Then I chuckled and remembered that spirits do not see my naked body, so I was able to quiet my human fears and listened to what he had to say.

"My name is John," he told me. "I died from an aneurysm, and my wife is coming to see you tomorrow. I am her boy. I am hers, she is mine and always will be."

That last bit was quite confusing to me. *Was he her husband or her son?*

Then John told me that his wife's name would be a version of Ann, and when I checked my schedule, I saw that I had both an Anne and an Anna booked for that day.

I asked the first client, Anne, "Do you understand the name John, who had an aneurysm?"

"No," she said, so I knew the message was meant for the other woman.

As soon as Anna arrived, I told her the words John had spoken earlier that morning: "I am her boy. I am hers, she is mine and always will be."

Anna began sobbing, "My husband, Johnny, died a month ago from an aneurysm. I always called him my boy. And we always said, 'I am yours and always will be.'"

Anna is still my client to this day, and we continue to have profound experiences with John.

During a different reading, I said to Anna, "I don't understand this, but John is talking about a cup of coffee." I don't drink coffee often, so it wouldn't typically pop into my head.

She laughed and said, "This morning when I was having my coffee, I told him that all I wanted him to say to you today was 'cup of coffee' for me to know he was really there."

This is just one example of how often John and Anna communicated before meeting with me. He would give me the exact information she asked him to tell me. Anna and John's loving bond continues beyond death, and witnessing it has been heartwarming.

❀ ❀ ❀

There have been many other instances in which a spirit provides the exact information a person asks for so they can let down their walls to receive their message. One time, it was a woman who wanted to speak to her mother.

I heard the whole story of her mother's difficult life as an immigrant. She worked as a seamstress and made doll clothes for a living. Although I hadn't heard this doll's name in many years, the name Kewpie came into my mind. The client broke down in tears when I said the word aloud. All she had wanted was for her mother to mention the Kewpie doll clothes that day, and she did.

Sometimes, I'm even called upon to relay something in a foreign language I don't know or say names aloud that I've never heard pronounced and don't know how to spell. While in a reading for a Japanese woman, I found myself singing a song in Japanese for her. It was an obscure song-like chant that her grandmother used to sing to her. Visitations like this continue to amaze me as they leave very little room for skepticism.

Physical Signs

Sometimes, physical manifestations occur during visitations. They are messages from spirits in physical form on earth. During one group reading, I spoke with my back to a large window.

"I have a spirit here who overdosed, the brother of someone in this room," I told the group. "He's saying he sends you hummingbirds to let you know he loves you. He isn't the hummingbird, but the hummingbird has been sent by him."

Then I noticed I'd lost everyone's attention. All eyes were drawn to the window instead. It turns out, unbeknownst to me, while I was talking, a hummingbird was hovering above my head on the other side of the window and then flew down and rested on the window frame.

While birds are a common sign, any animal may be a messenger from your loved ones in spirit. I was recently interviewed by Dr. Laura Berman on her podcast, *The Language of Love*. Her son-in-spirit, Sammy, came through to me while we recorded.

I asked her, "Does this mean anything to you? Your son is sending me a picture in my mind. What I see is a lizard doing push-ups."

She smiled, as she hadn't yet shared with anyone that she currently had a lizard at home, and that morning she saw it bending and straightening its legs like it was doing push-ups. We had a good laugh at Sammy sending her messages through a lizard!

Sammy then mentioned two distinct birds that had a significant impact. During the podcast, Dr. Berman didn't know what her son was referencing, but once we signed off, she realized, "After losing my son, two birds hit his bedroom window and fell to the ground."

I sometimes do readings in old, haunted Hollywood hotel rooms and post videos on my Instagram and TikTok accounts. We use a UV light that glows purple, the only color it can emit. Once, I began channeling a spirit who said to the present group, "I'd like to change the color of that light from purple to blue." Suddenly, the light turned blue, even though that was technologically impossible. Everyone was in shock! This was recorded on video, as well as various images of the spirits during these Hollywood adventures.

Communicating in a Coma

Sometimes I receive information from people when they are in a coma. It is an in-between state that enables them to communicate with me.

At times, it can be challenging to accurately connect with our own loved ones because we're too emotionally involved. This is true even for mediums. And so a friend, who is also a medium, called me one day about her cousin, who was like a sister to her. She wanted to know if I could obtain any information about whether her cousin would survive her bout with COVID-19.

Unfortunately, I could tell she would not survive, but I didn't want to say this to my friend. Instead I said, "The will of the soul is mighty."

She then asked me to do Reiki healing on her cousin from a distance. While I don't usually do so, I made an exception for her. During the healing, I heard the cousin tell me telepathically that she could hear her deceased sister and mother calling her from the other side. Still, her husband kept pulling her back energetically to earth. She said he was sitting on her right side, and she also gave me the names of the other people in the room. And there was one thing she really wanted them to know: her feet were very cold.

Since a coma is usually the only way someone who's still living can communicate with me in this way, I knew she must be in a coma. When I checked with my friend, she verified that she was, and everything I had been told during the Reiki session was spot-on. So, I let her know that her cousin's feet were cold.

"Oh my God, my sister and I were just texting about covering her feet!"

Her cousin fought the disease for another month or so before she crossed the vibrational veil.

Finding Justice

During a rather profound client session of mine, a mother came to me wanting to know if her son's death was accidental or if he had been lost to suicide. She was almost on the verge of killing herself because she felt she had to be with him and learn the truth.

"I have your son here with me, and he is with another baby, your other baby, and he wants you to know that they are both safe and happy. Does that make sense to you?"

"Wow, yes," she said. "I lost a baby a few years before my older son passed. Oh my God, how could you know that?"

"Your son wants you to know that it's really him, so he's telling me things only you would know. He also says he is very excited for his sister's upcoming wedding!"

The woman started to gently weep. From there, her son proceeded to provide many evidential details that the mother understood surrounding his death, including dates, times, and places. Once she knew that this was her son speaking, he addressed the main concern she walked in with.

"This is hard to say, but he is telling me that he did not kill himself. He is confirming that he was murdered, and he wants you to seek justice." He then named his assailant!

The mother took the information to the police. Eventually, they gathered enough evidence to put the perpetrator behind bars.

It was astonishing to me that a mystery could be solved, and justice served, from the afterlife. Later, I would dive more deeply into this work, known as forensic mediumship. (You'll learn more about this type of mediumship in Chapter 9.)

The Purpose behind the Visitations

The common message of all these stories is that *visitations from spirits help us heal*. When in the throes of profound grief, we may feel incredibly alone and isolated. We can even feel abandoned by our loved one who has passed, particularly in cases of suicide. And we certainly can feel abandoned by God. It's a lonely journey that can make people's lives difficult to bear. Our loved ones on the other side visit us to help us along on the agonizing grief journey. They want to help us heal by assuring us they are not gone and that the relationship continues. When they visit us, whether through dreams or signs or a medium, they are signaling to us that it is time for us to start our healing process.

They know that when we have a genuine experience of the afterlife and receive concrete evidence that our bond with them remains, we can then begin to accept their passing. This understanding helps us find peace, resolve our grief, and live better lives. It can be a source of comfort and hope to know that our loved ones are still with us in spirit, guiding and supporting us from beyond.

By acknowledging the continued relationships with those who have passed on, we can honor their memory and find the strength to face the challenges of life without them. The prolific writer Paulo Coelho said in his book *Aleph*, "Never. We never lose our loved ones. They accompany us; they don't disappear from our lives. We are merely in different rooms." And it's when we can have a firsthand peek into that "different room" that we are able to heal. My job as a medium is to help open the door.

Knowing these visitations are healing, I am often asked, "Why don't my deceased loved ones visit me more often?" The candid answer is that spirits want you to focus on life, not death. Here's an example: Those of us who have had a dream visitation from a loved one in spirit know how memorable that experience is. You *know* in your soul that it's not an ordinary dream—they were there with you. It feels so real, and you are so happy to be back together with them. Sadly, those dreams don't come very often but for a simple reason: If you knew the person you were deeply grieving would visit you every time you dreamed, would you ever get out of bed?

Our loved ones on the other side always visit us to help us heal and continue moving forward in our lives. They have no intention of keeping us in the vibration of depression and despair. They don't want us sad in bed; they want us back on our feet, smiling. Visitations are *always* for healing.

It's important to understand that mediums aren't the ones offering all the healing—mediums are *vessels* through which spirits bring the opportunity to heal. Clients need me to suit up for work and bring evidence of the afterlife. In truth, it's me asking spirits to suit up for work and bring evidence of the afterlife!

Because I am not in control, there isn't a day that goes by that I am not anxious to show up for work. *What if the loved ones in spirit don't come today? What if I'm wrong? What if I accidentally harm instead of heal today?* I occasionally have conversations with spirits about this when I'm deep in self-doubt and tell them I can't go to work that day. But they always reply, "Yes, Susan, you can; come back to us in an hour after your first session and see if you still feel the same way." Of course, after the session, I am reminded that my spirit team always shows up, just as I ultimately knew they would.

I know how important and delicate working with grieving people can be. I understand that I am not doing a significant portion of the healing; at the same time, I also know that I share the healing process as the conduit for Spirit. This means I must place all my trust in the spirit world to successfully do what I do. I can't say this is an easy job, but like most things that are difficult, the healing that takes place makes it a valuable and worthy deed.

Over the years, I have learned that there are many people who have been conditioned to believe mediumship to be somehow evil. Still, when I see people healing their deep-seated grief day after day in my office, I am clear that this is not a truth. Evil doesn't heal; it destroys, and forming connections with our loved ones on the other side is the greatest soother of grief I have ever witnessed. And it's important to note that having After-Death Communication does not require a medium. *Everyone* has spirit visitations—most of us either minimize them ("Oh, it was probably just a coincidence!") or fear exploring them deeper due to being thought of as crazy.

I believe there are people all over the world who experience visitations from loved ones in spirit but have never spoken a word about it for fear of rejection and judgment. In doing that, we shut ourselves off from Spirit and our loved ones on the other side who want to help us heal. As with anything, if we don't use it, what good is it to us? We can all tap into this part of ourselves, realize firsthand that we don't die, love lives forever, and begin transmuting our grief into gold.

I close this chapter with stories from my clients in their own words. It is so powerful when experiences are shared through the eyes of the person who lived it.

IN THEIR OWN WORDS:
Anna T.

I began seeing Susan after I lost the love of my life. I knew I needed something to give me hope for survival, and grief counselors were just not doing it for me. Susan connected with my husband immediately. She described him physically, told me specific personality traits, and described how he had passed and certain episodes that happened in the hospital while he was in a coma. She mentioned a special endearment that we would say to one another every day.

My lifeline had started. Susan was leading me out of the depths of depression. I realized what a gifted individual she is. She was really communicating with my husband, and life could go on for me. It would be hard, but I could do it.

I consider Susan not only a gifted medium but also a grief counselor and a dear friend. Each time we meet, it is always meaningful, and she continues to amaze me. For example, in another session, Susan told me that my husband had met a young man, Ty, whom he helped pass over to the other side. She said we both knew this man casually and that he died of a brain aneurysm just as my husband had. She relayed that Ty was concerned for his parents and wanted them to know he was safe. He didn't want them to worry. Susan said Ty's parents were Cathy and Ralf, spelling the name out for me, R-A-L-F. I wasn't sure who she meant, but I assured her I would look into it.

That night, my friend Tina called crying and asked me to pray for her daughter's ex-boyfriend Tyler. He was a healthy, vivacious athlete who had just passed the day before from a brain aneurysm, and they were beside themselves with grief and anguish.

I asked Tina for his parents' names. She said, "Cathy and Ralf." I learned Ralf is from Europe, hence the spelling. Tyler's parents were in the deepest despair, yet their son was reaching out to them, making sure we spelled Ralf correctly so they would know it was really him and he was still with them. I shared Ty's message with Tina, and in turn, Tina shared it with Cathy and Ralf.

Susan is a gifted, loving soul who blesses people with her gifts. With the help of Spirit, Susan has given these people a lifeline of hope and solace without ever meeting them.

IN THEIR OWN WORDS:
Sunny M.

I lost my daughter, Kasey, on July 23, 2020. The trauma of the grief I was experiencing was almost too much to bear, especially alone. She had been my best friend from even before she was born.

Two months after her death, I ran across an article about a medium in California, Susan Grau. The article was by someone who had "tested" mediums and ranked them according to their ability to give specific evidence—telling the client things no one but the departed loved one would know, things no one could look up. Susan Grau was at the top of the list. So I went to her website and signed up for both a grief workshop and a 50-minute mediumship reading.

On the day of the reading, I was anxious and skeptical. I'm an attorney and a keen observer of people and patterns, and I have this profound need for actual proof—of nearly everything. I withhold judgment until I'm thoroughly convinced of guilt or innocence, or in this case, a medium's true ability.

My daughter and I were both believers in the unseen world. We talked about how we were sure our passed relatives had "visited" us in dreams and that we saw coincidences as the Universe's synchronicity. But neither of us had any psychic abilities, nor had we had actual readings connecting us with the spirit world. After my sweet Kasey's death, I had to know she was still with me.

Susan began the reading by saying she "had a male and female spirit" and that "the male spirit was saying he had been there to help the female spirit cross over." She wanted me to know he "was with her." I assumed it might be my father, who had died on Kasey's birthday years before, but as though reading my mind, Susan said, "She's saying it's her uncle, so if you think it's your father, it isn't. She says it's her uncle." Then Susan said, "I see an umbilical cord. She's saying 'Mom' . . . Is this your mom? Or are you her mom?"

I was stunned and could barely form the words, but I said, "She's my daughter." From that point, it was like a floodgate of information poured forth. Although the cause of her death was known to me—a drug overdose—whether it was intentional or not wasn't clear. Susan told me the exact combination of drugs that killed my daughter. I had only just received the medical examiner's report with this information in it the day before; no one was privy to these details except the Chicago medical examiner and myself.

Susan told me repeatedly that my daughter was saying, "It was an accident, Mom. I didn't mean to do this to you." She described the scene where she was found and by whom, and more importantly for me, what her final moments were like. "I just fell asleep, Mom; there was no pain, and I wasn't afraid."

She said her uncle and her dog were there immediately for her when she crossed over. Susan said, "I see a larger dog. An 'M' name? Mac? Mac? Mac? I love that music! I love that music."

I stopped her even though she continued offering more information and said, "Wait! What music? What music are you talking about?"

Susan said, "I don't know. . . . She was talking about her dog and then said, 'I love that music!'"

My daughter had named her big yellow Lab "Mac," after her favorite band, Fleetwood Mac. Mac had died a few years before. I was now just stunned, and tears were falling down my face. This was precisely what I had hoped for—tangible evidence that Kasey was still here; though her body was gone, her consciousness and spirit lived on.

"She's singing that song. . . . Oh, what is it? You know . . ." Susan began humming the tune and singing the lyrics. Before Susan could reach the next line, I yelled out, "'Landslide'! That's 'Landslide.'" It was Kasey's favorite song—the song we played and sang at her military service and the lyrics I referenced in her obituary and on her grave marker.

This was merely the beginning of my journey through the grief this horrible loss caused me to experience, but it was a decisive turning point. Further sessions with Susan have helped heal my soul, where years of therapy just couldn't. I jokingly refer to her as my soul therapist because, through this challenging landscape of the last two years, the hours spent with Susan have enabled me to overcome what was once unceasing, searing pain. My friendship with Susan has given me needed direction through this foreign territory of heartbreaking sadness, regret, and unrelenting sorrow. It is now helping me grow and accept these losses and disappointments as part of my journey in this lifetime.

IN THEIR OWN WORDS:
Katherine E.

For the past few years, my mother has been stuck in grief from the sudden loss of her sister, who was taken by breast cancer. Looking for any way to provide my mom some peace, I found Susan on Yelp and immediately made an appointment.

No words can describe the peace Susan gave my mother. The peace she has been yearning for. My aunt, along with several others, came through. It was like a family reunion. Each person gave my mother the love and peace she had been looking for. Everything Susan said resonated with my mom, if not in the moment, days later.

After the appointment, when I looked at my mother throughout the day, I almost didn't recognize her. Happiness just radiated off her. Happiness I haven't seen in so long. Years of sadness and questions completely lifted. Since that day, my mom says she is still walking on air.

I cannot thank Susan enough for giving me my mother back. My mom kept exclaiming, "How?" Because she met Susan, her life is forever changed. Well, so is mine.

IN THEIR OWN WORDS:
Pattie S.

My brother and I went to see Susan after losing our sister. We could tell instantly by her kindness that she cared and was very spiritually connected. We were not sure how we felt about mediums but wanted answers. I did my research before choosing her. Susan had amazing Yelp reviews so we booked an appointment. We were hoping that we would get the answers that we desperately needed. Well, we did, and then some! She was very warm and gentle in her approach, which eased our fears. She proceeded to tell us my sister's favorite song and that it was sung at her celebration of life.

We were stunned but continued to be skeptical. Well, that skepticism went right out the door as she continued to share the nickname we lovingly called my sister. Without any prompts from us, Susan said that my sister's death wasn't a suicide but accidental, which was our actual question and reason for wanting to see a medium. That alone was so healing for myself and my brother.

She also said that her dog passed right after her, and they were together. She then told us our sister's favorite location was a reef off Hawaii's coast and that we had spread her ashes there. What!? She followed with the information that my sister was there with us while we spread her ashes. She said my sister was telling her she gave us this message by way of showing us a dolphin while we were releasing them. We knew she couldn't possibly know that. My brother and I were blown away, shocked, and excited. Susan spent the next 30 minutes telling us how happy my sister was and all the signs that she was sending, all of which we had experienced since my sister died. I felt a sense of peace as she was talking.

Whatever skepticism we had about the legitimacy of mediums was gone. When we were leaving, Susan shared that we would see an owl that evening, not just any owl but one that would sit in the tree next to our house and hoot toward our home. To my surprise, my family saw and heard that owl right where she said. Seeing Susan was the best choice my brother and I made. It felt like a year of grief therapy in one hour. Thank you, Susan, for the best and most healing experience ever.

INTEGRATION MOMENT
You Have to Feel It to Heal It

Grief over the death of a loved one is one of the most powerful emotions in the world and can temporarily tear a life apart. It is one of the greatest hardships that we are asked to overcome during this human experience, and the purpose of visitations from our loved ones in spirit is *always* to help us step onto the path of healing. We often want to bury or numb our grief, but when we look at it head-on, true transformation occurs—in other words, we have to feel it to heal it.

Choose any of the prompts below to explore your experience with grief, spirit visitations, and where you currently are on your healing journey. What is your grief story, whether it be the loss of an immediate family member, a pet, or a friend? Who have you loved so much you've grieved over their loss, and what has been the most challenging part of the loss for you? What steps have you taken to begin healing?

- How have you grown from experiencing deep grief? How have you transmuted your grief into gold?

- Have you had a visitation from a loved one in spirit? If so, have you put the visitation down on paper? It is something you can return to when you forget they're around.

- What type of spirit visitations have you had? Were they dreams, physical manifestations, a mediumship session, or a gut-knowing that your loved one was there? How have these visitations helped you heal on your grief journey?

- What do you believe about the afterlife? Where do you feel your deceased loved ones are? What do you think comes next after this life?

Chapter Exercises

After a loss, how often do we say, "I just know they're here; I can feel them." I hear this common theme from others, and it helps them process the loss. It is a way to visualize our loved ones and to feel a sense of peace, even for a moment. It can be a powerful analgesic to calm our fears and pain.

When the anxiety creeps in like an unwanted visitor, I ask myself this question often, as I am sure you do: "How is it possible for me to survive this pain? How is that possible?" And yet, against all odds, we survive!

My mantra for my own loss is, *"I can't, they can, let them!"*
Whenever I start to panic, I say: *I can't* do this without a connection,
they can connect with me, and I will *let them* show me. It's not a
solution to the pain, yet it helps me trust they are there, walking
this journey of loss with me in some unseen way.

Try the following exercises to help you feel more connected
to your loved one:

- Spend time with others in your family discussing what each
  person feels the afterlife looks like and what your loved ones
  may be doing while they are there.

- This may be a time for deeper reflection. Take a drive to your
  loved one's favorite place. Ask them to help you visualize
  what they are doing and seeing. Write down everything that
  you receive.

- Spend time alone in a dimly lit room. Ask your loved one to
  show you a clear sign or a vision. It takes time for spirits to
  figure out the "right" method for reaching out on request.
  Be patient with those in the spirit world; it takes them time.
  Hold a photo or two in your hand. Looking at pictures helps
  us connect with our loved ones and often helps us remember the
  ways in which that person still influences our lives. Take time
  to remember the conversations that passed between you both
  when they were on this planet.

- Remember to bring memories of your deceased loved
  one into the conversation at family gatherings only when
  you feel ready. What would their opinion be regarding the
  subject being discussed? How might they have reacted to
  what is being shared?

Remember, keeping them alive within us becomes easier as
time goes on. Don't push yourself beyond your limits. Grief is a
powerful force. Be easy and gentle with yourself.

CHAPTER 8

Signs from Our Loved Ones

Throughout my years as a medium, I have so many treasured stories from clients, and I have witnessed many miracles where spirits have communicated through me to let their loved ones know that a sign would soon be sent to them. If you find yourself questioning this, rest assured that you are not alone. All of us who have had a loss have questioned the validity when a sign from a loved one is given, but at the end of the day, these signs help many in their grief, and that is what makes them more than just valid; it makes the signs powerful and necessary for healing.

A Fatherly Hug from a Stranger

"Your father, Ed, is telling me he will send you a message through a stranger," I told my client Meghan. Her father's spirit was an unexpected communication, as he hadn't yet crossed over but was in a deep coma.

Later, Meghan called me and said that visiting hours had ended at the ICU, where her father remained. I felt an urgency to remind Meghan again, "Your father will give you a message that you won't be expecting through a stranger."

As the day ended, she stopped to get gas after leaving the hospital. The man behind the counter smiled and said hello to her, then asked, "Do you have a dad nearby? Your eyes remind me of a nice man who comes here before work in his truck."

Although distraught, she remembered what I said to her earlier and replied, "Yes, I do."

He then asked, "Is the truck dark green? I believe his name is Ed!"

"That's probably my dad!" Shocked that this stranger brought up her father but still unsure if he was the messenger I mentioned earlier, she said, "Hi, my name's Meghan—it's nice to meet you." Then she left to put gas in her car.

This kind man followed her out and said in a soft voice similar to her dad's, "Megs . . . Megs, you look like you could use a hug." She was unsure how to react because her dad was the only person to call her "Megs." To her surprise, he wrapped his arms around her in a strong, long hug, just like her father always hugged her.

Before releasing her, the gentleman whispered, "Don't forget who you are, Megs." This was the exact phrase her dad always used when she needed loving support.

When we spoke again, she told me the whole story and said, "I got the message! You were right! You said a stranger would give me a message from my dad! My dad is out of his body! You were right!"

I was elated that her father had come to her; I listened to every detail with the same awe she was feeling. I then decided to ask her about a name that I heard: "Meghan, what does *'beja'* mean? Your father keeps saying, 'I love you, *'beja.'"*

"Susan! My dad only calls me Megs or Bella; you're saying it exactly how my dad does, in the same accent!" Shocked, she explained that in traditional Spanish "bella" means beautiful, but in Castilian, the accent sounds like *b-eh-ja.* She shouted excitedly that her father was beginning to give her signs that she could recognize.

Later that evening, I received another message, so I texted Meghan, "Does the song 'Nights in White Satin' have importance to your father?"

The following morning from the ICU, Meghan sent me a photo of her dad's phone screen with the last song he played on it—"Nights in White Satin" by The Moody Blues.

She replied, "There's *no way* you could know this! *How? Susan!* My Dad is communicating these signs through you!"

Meghan began documenting each sign her father would send, from hummingbirds to butterflies, hawks, owls, shooting stars, songs on the radio, signs on billboards, flickering lights, doors opening by themselves, and constant angel numbers—like getting the feeling to check the time at 11:11 and receiving calls or seeing license plates with the digits 1111. The signs were endless, in every direction. Meghan must have sent me over 100 photos and videos in three weeks.

I woke up on October 2, 2022, at 3:33 A.M.—more angel numbers!—and found Ed's spirit in my room, telling me he had passed. As I began typing a text to Meghan, I received a message from her confirming he'd passed.

I told Meghan that her father wanted her to have a silver ring that belonged to him and had to do with the ocean. As her family arrived at her father's home to begin sorting through Ed's belongings, on his nightstand was a silver ring with small ocean waves engraved around the band. It was a gift Meghan gave her father for his birthday when she was a child that she hadn't seen in years.

I assured Meghan her father would be giving her a visitation soon. Three nights later, Meghan received the profound healing she desperately needed, a life-changing visitation from Ed while she slept. She called me from her bed, *"Susan, you were right; oh, Susan, it felt so real!* It felt like my soul traveled to another dimension to have closure from my dad! It felt just as *real* as being awake!"

She shared every detail of her visitation, and the healing was beautiful. It was wonderful to see the power of the spirit world and to know her father gave her what she needed to begin the healing process.

The Blue Bird

I was on the phone, giving a reading to a woman in Sydney, Australia, when I received an image of a beautiful bird. "Your mother tells me she will send you a bird. I *see* a bird of some kind; it appears to be a shiny, bright blue." I described it in detail based on her mother's image.

"I know just what bird you're talking about!" she said. "It's a very special bird found in Australia called the splendid fairywren."

"It is? I don't know anything about the birds there. But she's telling me she will send you this bird."

Not long after her reading, my client became very ill, which led to an infection in her lungs. Her fever spiked so high that she worried she might die, so she asked her mother for help. Her mother came to her in her dreams and handed her a splendid fairywren. She asked again for help with her severe body pain, and again the bird was offered to her.

When the woman awoke in the morning, her fever had broken. A few hours later, at her window, she saw the same bird that had been in her dreams. She told me later she *felt* this was a sign from her mom and that she was aiding in her recovery. She now felt more peaceful about her mom's death and was sure she was visiting her.

The Signs I Needed

Now I want to share a profoundly personal experience of receiving a much-needed sign at an extremely painful point in *my* life. When my mother attempted suicide, she did not die from that attempt; she died four days later from complications from the attempt. I spent four days in a hospice watching my mom, blue and bloated, die a slow death. It was the most horrific thing I've been through in my life, and I've been through a lot.

Prior to this, both of my brothers had also taken their own lives, so I felt as if suicide was haunting me at this point. Why was everyone around me choosing to leave me? The cumulative pain became debilitating once my mother attempted to leave me too. I felt rejected. I was struggling deeply with these all-consuming thoughts of abandonment by the people I love while simultaneously being plagued with thoughts of what my mother was going through.

In my darkest moment, I asked my father, who had already crossed, to confirm that he was with her and would help her peacefully exit. Only a moment later, a butterfly appeared out of nowhere and hit me directly between my eyes! I might have dismissed this sign as a coincidence in the past, but this felt different; it felt spiritual in nature. Butterflies have always had a special place in my heart and have been a personal sign for me. A spirit will communicate with us in forms *we* can understand, so at that moment, I knew my father was reassuring me that he would be there for my mother during her transition. This sign helped slightly ease an otherwise horrendous situation.

I had experienced so much death and grief in my life by this point, and I dealt with these difficult topics every day as a medium. But my mother's death was *the one* death that brought me completely to my knees, and I didn't think I would ever get back up. And for a long time, I didn't. It was the most devastating experience of my life; it unraveled me to the very core of my existence. And the fact that my mother had *chosen* to leave me made the deep pain that much more unbearable. Not only was I deeply grieving, I was simultaneously feeling all the horrible feelings suicide brings with it: guilt, betrayal, rejection.

When someone we love chooses to kill themselves, we feel responsible in some form. We torment ourselves with the "what if's": What if I wouldn't have said this, what if I would have said that, what if I would have paid more attention? Suicide has a way of making you feel like you failed that person. Like you let them down in the most primal of ways. It has taken me a long time to understand that I am not responsible for my mother's—or anyone else's—choice to end their life. No "what if" in the world can override a person's free will. I carried that guilt for a long time until I learned it was not mine to carry.

When my mother eventually passed, my grief was made worse by a particularly terrible dream I had: I saw my mother walking down a hallway, opening and closing doors, obviously lost and trying to find her way. When I called her name, she turned to me and morphed into a very frightening entity.

Upon waking, I was completely distressed. I had never experienced anything like that before—for the first time in my life, I didn't know if a dream was real or not. I tried to communicate with my mother to make sure she was okay, but I wasn't able to connect with her.

I continued my attempt over many days afterward, becoming more and more concerned because she still wasn't communicating with me. Then I realized that, even though I am a medium, she might need to contact me through someone else because my grief was blocking communication. So I decided to visit a trusted medium in order to have a clear channel to speak with her.

"I need to know my mom is safe and secure on the other side," I told the medium, Colleen, after explaining my dream and my inability to connect with her since.

"Your mother is here and she is safe, Susan," Colleen assured me. "Your dream only symbolizes your fear around your mother's death, since it was traumatic, and you are plagued with the 'what if's.' But she assures you now that she is not lost, she is safely on the other side, and she will send you a hawk as a clear message that she is safe and that she loves you."

I shared my uncertainty. Although hawks were unusual where I lived, seeing one would not convince me enough to believe it was a sign from my mother.

She replied, "She tells me she will show you the hawk in an undeniable way."

I was still reasonably skeptical, but I was willing to see. I needed to hear from my mom.

It wasn't normal for me not to trust, but like all of us, I also live a human experience; I, too, doubt at times. Especially in deep grief.

Five days later, a neighbor called me outside. I hadn't told him anything about this conversation, so you can imagine my surprise when he showed me a hawk sitting in the tree, actually *staring* into my home. Still, I wasn't entirely convinced.

The next day my husband called me outside to tell me a hawk was sitting on our fence looking into our back window. My husband tried to scare it away, but the hawk stayed right where it was. It seemed almost *fixated* on me. I finally gave in and said, "Okay, I *believe!*" When I said this, the hawk flew away and we never saw it again.

Receiving Your Own Signs

This amazing experience with my mother opened my eyes and revealed how hard our loved ones work to send us messages from the spirit world. They communicate in a way that makes even the most skeptical people acknowledge the possibility of life after death. The hawk is my reminder that even after crossing over, they can still show us that they haven't left us behind. It is also a reminder of how essential and important it is to trust and believe in the signs we receive and to remain open to the realm of *infinite wisdom*.

Our loved ones provide us with comfort and direction during difficult times in our lives, guiding and offering us solace. The types of signs they send are usually those that connect with our souls individually, but some signs are more common than others. I'll share common signs later in this chapter.

On the other side, they see us grieving because they are no longer with us physically. They see us lost and feeling abandoned and alone, and they want to send signs to remind us they are there. When we remain open to the signs our loved ones are sending, we can feel their infinite love for us, which they hope will offer us strength to continue walking our intended paths (*remember the Yellow Brick Road!*).

Do you have to be a medium or see one to receive these signs and messages from your loved ones? No! Consulting a medium is a helpful way to hear from those who have left this earthly plane, but it is far from the only way. *All* of us are capable of receiving messages firsthand. It first requires being open—specifically, opening your heart. Of course, this is easier said than done in a logic-obsessed world.

You are only as receptive to them as your own limiting beliefs allow. As the Sioux Tribe saying goes: "The longest journey you will make in your life is from your head to your heart." But, as with most painstaking spiritual pilgrimages, the rewards of committing to this long journey are priceless. Are you ready to take the first step?

Tapping into Your Heart Intelligence

Your heart has its own unique intelligence. The neural system in the head, known as the master brain or "big brain," is considered our intelligence hub since it sends information and messages to the body through several pathways: neurological, biochemical, biophysical, and energetic; however, the most interesting findings are that our heart demonstrates its own particular intelligence.

The heart's neural system comprises over *40,000* neurons and uses this pathway to communicate with the brain, thus it's called "the little brain." The ongoing neural connection between the brain (mind) and heart creates a solid reliance and strong bond, intertwining our thoughts with our emotions.

The heart constantly relays insights to the brain, awakening new perspectives and emotions. It has a plethora of information to share and eagerly wants to be detected and heard. The heart communicates more with the brain than the other way around! That being the case, it's important to note that the heart's wisdom in our lives is a dynamic confirmation that our intuition and feelings are valid and essential to our overall well-being. With wise guidance in all decisions, the heart's intuitive nudges assist us to better understand ourselves and the world around us.

Life is full of challenging situations that are primarily out of our control. The heart's intelligence helps us realign with Spirit, ensure better relationships, sort out difficulties with discernment, and discover new levels of personal growth. As we learn to tap into this *knowing*, known as innate knowledge, we can experience a more positive, harmonious, and balanced life, which is important for ourselves and those we share our lives with. The heart has a meaningful impact on our physical, emotional, and mental state as it carries an ongoing dialogue with the mind.

The heart is the primary organ to develop in the embryo with an electromagnetic field so intense that it surpasses beyond our skin by a radius of three to four feet, creating a powerful magnetism all around us in a 360-degree circumference. The magnificent and beautiful magnetism of the heart is felt by spirits and humans alike. Its powerful strength and unseen enigmatic output are still being discovered.

Both ancient and modern philosophers believe that the heart is the "seat of the soul"—the secure, intuitive resting place. The famous phrase "follow your heart" does contain some practical advice; it means to be aware of the messages you receive and to tap into your intuition, your love, and soul because it's essential in being receptive to the spirit world. Our intuition is the "voice of the soul."

The most important things in life can't be seen with the naked eye. To be closer to the eternal, you need to be closer to your heart. Here is a little secret that I have always understood: "The only way to see things for what they are is through your heart, not your eyes."

Even though what I'm saying seems mysterious and mystical, consider what the renowned thinker and scientist Albert Einstein said: "Don't let your brain interfere with your heart." Einstein understood the balance between the mind and the heart. Over time, I have realized that we become more connected to our authentic selves when we tap into the intelligence of the heart.

If you are a spiritual seeker, the above is important to understand the key to reaching your true spiritual potential. You can cultivate a balance between rational thinking and the heart by quieting your mind and opening the intuitive knowing. Integrating the heart and mind connection to your spiritual *knowing* is the dance of expanding your awareness of the afterlife.

Now that we have learned the importance of being aware of our heart's intuitive messages and the understanding that stepping into the seat of the soul is essential to connecting with spirits, it's time to begin. The first step to learning anything new is willingness; learning to form a direct relationship with your loved ones in spirit is no different.

Overcoming Limiting Beliefs

For successful communication with the other side, you must be willing to learn the tools necessary. You must be ready to practice and have patience as you learn. Simply, you must be willing to *try*.

Spirits do not interfere with your free will, so if you are adamant that you lack the ability to communicate with the unseen world, you more than likely never will. But I assure you, everyone has the ability to be creative, and everyone has the ability to communicate with their loved ones in spirit—both are birthrights to us all. It's not that we don't have the ability; it's that we don't *believe* we have the ability.

Limiting beliefs can take many forms and vary per person. For instance, some may believe they are not gifted or connected enough and that only certain people have the ability to communicate with spirits. Others have fears of the unknown or are skeptical of anything *seen* beyond the physical realm—ideals of danger or impossibility. These beliefs can create emotional and mental obstacles, obstructing, delaying, or even blocking communication between the living and the spirit world. They can prevent subtle signs of communication and messages, which their loved ones may be trying to send to them daily.

In my work as an intuitive medium, I have seen first-hand how limiting beliefs can interfere with the spirit world's communication. It's a part of my intuitive practice to help others overcome, process, and identify their limiting beliefs. My objective is to create a safe and supportive environment through gentle encouragement where my clients can receive communication from their loved ones. These practices help many overcome preconceived concepts or fears. I continue to witness that, as communication with the spirit world becomes more accessible to them, it also becomes more meaningful.

It's essential to remember that the more faith or belief one invests in the unseen world, the more it reveals itself. We can all understand our physical world and the realities around us, but the unseen world requires a measure of expected and unexpected possibilities.

Author Dr. Wayne Dyer often said, "You'll see it when you believe it!" That means you can make your life *all* you want it to be if you can just *believe* it! Spirit does not push you to believe if you're not ready. It takes a lot of time to process grief and the emotions that arise from the loss experience. Your readiness to venture out and believe will appear in your own time. Develop patience and practice skills. Mastery requires patience and dedication. Spirit communication is no exception; everything becomes more evident as your awareness is heightened.

Raising Our Vibration

The spirit realm vibrates at a much higher frequency than we do here on earth. To connect with the other side, the most important thing we must master is raising the state of our vibration. Doing so will give us a clearer sense of what spirits are trying to communicate.

Our emotions determine vibrations, and each emotion equates to a different level of energetic frequency. Love is the highest vibration, while one of the lower energetic vibrations is fear followed closely by heavier emotions such as anger, grief, and shame.

Our feelings are valid, and we must move through them, both the positive and the negative. Avoidance of heavier emotions isn't the aim; instead, move into them and then allow these emotions to express and transmute. Doing whatever we can to work through painful emotions and elevate our frequency is vital in connecting to our hearts. That, in turn, creates a stronger connection to the spirit consciousness.

Our loved ones can pick up on and connect with our energy more easily as our vibration increases. You can raise your vibration by getting a good rest, practicing an attitude of gratitude, playing music, laughing, dancing, or doing anything as an act of true self-care or joy. And, of course, I'd be remiss if I didn't mention meditation, one of the most powerful methods of elevating your vibration. Meditation can help you quiet your mind and calm your emotions. Doing so makes you more receptive to telepathic messages your loved one may be trying to communicate to you.

The saying "good vibes only" is not just a positive phrase; it holds significance in our life journey. However, as suffering is inherent to human existence, achieving this goal is not always possible. In truth, it can be virtually impossible to feel joy when we are in the midst of painful, heart-numbing grief.

Grief is a dense vibration and can act as a wall, making contact with the person you are grieving difficult. Be patient and easy on yourself if this is the state you are currently in. You are in the most painful, vulnerable condition when grieving. You must keep the awareness that we don't decide when we are done with grief—the intensity of grief decides when it is done with us. Don't *force* solutions.

Give yourself grace and time to understand how to connect. Remember that *forced* solutions are never *good* solutions. Your connection will happen if you remain committed. Sometimes it takes a while, and that's perfectly normal. Learn to trust that it will happen, then allow the process. The next chapter will delve deeper into the topic of grief but know for now that if you are currently experiencing it, it's imperative to be gentle with yourself and show yourself compassion during this difficult time.

However, it's also important to understand that allowing moments of joy amidst grief can help bring your loved ones in the spirit world closer to you. That's not to say you should deny or suppress your emotions of sorrow. Instead, attempt to search for moments of positivity and comfort when possible.

If you are currently in a grief cycle, giving yourself grace and compassion is essential. Even while grieving, feeling joy and allowing yourself to laugh will help bring your loved ones closer. Think of a person busy in another room in the same house you are in—as they hear laughter and music, they want to come out to see what is happening! That is the vibration we want to send to our loved ones in spirit. Of course, never deny your pain and your need to mourn. However, it is okay to feel other emotions besides grief, even for a moment.

During grief, it can be challenging to notice messages or signs from your loved ones. But that doesn't mean they aren't trying to communicate with you; it simply means that your grief is so low in vibration it could be getting in the way of sensing them. Their goal is to bring you comfort and to remind you that they are there and you are loved. They will use any means necessary to do so, even if that means speaking to someone else because they can't get through to you at the time. They may talk to your loved one, a relative, a friend, or even a stranger. They want you to know that they love and cherish you. Remember, the truth is they are only a heartbeat away, watching and patiently waiting to communicate with you.

The Differences between Spirit Guides and Loved Ones

I'm consistently asked common questions such as, "Is it really my loved one coming to me?" "How do I know it's really them?" "What's the difference between a spirit guide or some other entity that might be coming in?" "Is it true that we get optimistic messages from our spirit guides, thinking it is our loved ones?" So let's discuss how to discern the differences between guides and loved ones, as it is imperative in communicating effectively with your family and friends on the other side.

Spirit guides are appointed by our souls before we are born to help us on our journey. They are with us to give us guidance, drawing our attention toward the positive during our entire life—to keep us on our path. They also seek to protect us from our negative choices, thoughts, and deeds. They communicate with us through *telepathic* thoughts for the most part but have been known to come in dreams and meditation as well. Unlike a deceased relative or friend, a spirit guide has been appointed by us to *guide* us during our lifetime. While they can't prevent us from making poor choices, nor are they meant to do so, they can sometimes *steer* us from those poor choices and try to lead us toward better ones.

There is a difference between receiving messages from spirit guides and from departed loved ones. Both provide valuable details and information, but they have different intentions and communication methods. Our spirit guides usually offer guidance and advice to help us find our way through life's challenges, while our loved ones offer us reassurances that they are still very much alive, and both communications can provide comfort and healing to the person experiencing the loss.

Our loved ones, now in spirit, tend to find ways to let us know that they are still with us, that love never ends, and that this love continues beyond our physical realm. They characteristically communicate their presence in our tangible world by leaving coins, feathers, words, numbers, or meaningful objects in our path. They might turn up in lifelike dreams or even send telepathic messages, evoking a feeling of love, support, and guidance. They may not be able to convey specific advice but knowing that they are still with us and that love transcends time and space can be reassuring during difficult times and bring us a sense of continuity and peace.

The unseen world is vast and works in unison with our physical world to bring us to a greater understanding of who we are and what our purpose is on earth. The messages we receive from departed loved ones or spirit guides should be approached with an open mind and heart. Trusting in these messages and markers can help us on this spiritual journey, guide us toward inner peace, and help us reach a greater understanding of *our* interconnectedness.

Regarding communication, I have had personal encounters as well as the *honor* of listening to and documenting countless experiences from clients who have been able to tap into these messages that are far too detailed or specific to be a coincidence. These forms of communication can be highly personal and unique to the relationship experienced in the natural world. The key is being open to recognizing and receiving these messages for what they are.

A passed-on loved one's presence may feel familiar or comfortable. You may sense a *knowing* or relive a memory of a picture, moment, voice, or scent. It's good practice to assume that these communications are occurring for a reason and insert some level of trust into the experience because their intent is usually love, comfort, and guidance. In contrast, a spirit guide does not carry or bring that *familiar* feeling or comfort level. That is how you distinguish between loved ones who have passed on or spirit guides.

Ways Our Loved Ones Communicate

Departed loved ones can no longer communicate through language like they used to do in their daily lives, so they may reach out through symbols, pictures, signs, songs, dreams, the manipulation of electricity or radio frequency, or making their presence known through touch, sound, smell, and in some cases speaking through other people or the alertness in animals. Though everyone's communication with the spirit world is unique to them, below are some common ways that our loved ones like to communicate with us from the other side:

— **Sensing their presence**: Sensing an unseen presence is an intuitive way of knowing that spirit is near you. You carry an *inner knowing* that you are not alone in the room. You can just feel it. Without physically *seeing* anything or anyone, you simply just know. You may tune in to their emotional state or sense their presence beside you, wanting to share and communicate. Then as fast as it arrives, it's gone.

These instances can easily be written off as nothing, but I promise you, it is something. Allow yourself the opportunity to trust and lean in to these moments, and these visits will begin happening more frequently and become more recognizable. *Sensing* their presence and acknowledging it makes room for even more communication.

— **Fragrance:** Have you ever experienced the *scent* of a deceased loved one's cologne or perfume? The smell of their favorite food or flower? Their flavor of tobacco smoke when no one nearby is smoking? Whatever the fragrance, when it comes from a spirit, it comes out of nowhere with no obvious point of origin. Spirits use all our senses to communicate; smell is no exception. The challenging part is *making sense of our senses.*

— **Temperature changes:** Dramatic temperature changes in a room are also a common sign that a spirit is nearby. If you feel a blast of cold air out of nowhere or a corner of your room is suddenly much colder than the rest of the otherwise temperate room, spirits are likely near you. It's what I call "the chill factor," and I always feel it during my mediumship sessions. Why does this happen? One theory is that whatever energy the spirit needs is pulled from the area that they are in—heat energy is transferred and the lack of heat results in cold. Whatever the scientific reason, cold blasts out of nowhere *do* mean spirits are near you, I can attest to that! So don't disregard when you get the chills while thinking about or talking about someone you love who's deceased—it means they hear you and are near you.

— **Music:** Have you ever been thinking about someone who has passed, and then a song that reminds you of them—that either you shared or that they loved—starts playing out of the blue? Immediately you *sense* that they are with you . . . because they are. Maybe the song even follows you, and you start to hear it everywhere, too often for it to be a coincidence. Remember, music is one of the languages of the spirit world, and they love to send messages through this medium that both worlds share.

— **Orbs:** Have you ever seen, out of the corner of your eye, some kind of shadow or blinking ball of light? Perhaps you don't see it in real time but in a photograph you have just taken. Or maybe in the baby monitor, you see an orb hovering over your child's crib, seemingly suspended in space, watching over your child.

Materialists will tell you that these are optical illusions or dust. Still, anyone with a spiritual eye will assure you that many are, in fact, spirits *revealing* themselves to us visually. If you ever go to a place known for its paranormal activity and take pictures, you will see plenty of orbs in your snapshots, and there is nothing coincidental or imaginary about it. In addition to orbs, sometimes you may make out the shape of a loved one in a photo—they absolutely love to join in on family photos!

— **Apparitions:** When revealing themselves, spirits sometimes show themselves as partial or complete apparitions. Apparition means "an unusual or unexpected sight." Seeing an apparition is rare, but when you see one, all of your doubt regarding the spirit world and your deceased loved one's continued existence vanishes. Apparitions look like a hologram, as though they are standing right before you, so close you could nearly touch them. Sometimes gone in a flash and other times lingering in your sight for some time, the apparition spirit will always appear healthy and luminous.

— **Touch:** Spirits communicate with us through every one of our senses, including touch. Have you ever felt a loving touch, poke, or pressure somewhere on your body? You might turn around and think you're going crazy because there is no one around that you can see! But of course, someone is about—and it's a spirit, saying hello.

— **Electrical interference and material movement:**
Lights flashing on and off, the radio changing stations, pictures or other items seemingly out of nowhere falling off shelves—these material manifestations are common ways of spirits communicating with us. Yes, they can catch us off guard and freak us out but know that your loved ones are never trying to scare you. Often, the items moved are related to the deceased, perhaps a picture of them or something that belonged to them, letting you know they are right there with you. Someone I know had flickering lights in every room in her house shortly after her mother died!

— **Talking to our children:** Have you ever noticed your toddler playing, laughing, and chatting with *themselves*? Imaginary friends aren't so imaginary, let me tell you! You might even hear the child mention the name or nickname of your deceased loved one or identify them in a picture even though they have never met them.

Children remain very close to the spirit world, making a *reliable* communication pathway. It would do us a lot of good to start listening to them with an open mind and to believe them when they share what they see and hear. Connected children love to play with their spirit friends—*trust me, I know!*

— **Symbolism:** One of the most common ways for loved ones in spirit to communicate with us is via *symbols*. They often send us signs that represent something we would understand. Common symbols that spirits send include butterflies, feathers, rainbows, coins with meaningful dates, consistent numbers, and birds of all sorts. But remember that it can be anything significant to them or you, so don't limit your thinking.

Whatever the sign, it typically appears out of nowhere. The importance lies in how these items manifest. For example, suppose you notice that a hummingbird is now regularly showing up at the exact spot where you and your husband used to have your coffee and morning chats. In that case, this experience is much more significant than simply spotting a hummingbird in a tree nearby. The former may be a *sign* of your husband's presence or a message from the spirit world, whereas the latter is just a common occurrence in nature.

— **Through an evidential medium:** A medium can communicate with a loved one in spirit and give *evidence* that they still exist and are in your life even after death. This evidence should be so clear that it helps you identify, beyond a shadow of a doubt, the soul who is coming through. *Knowing* it is your loved one communicating is as important as the messages being shared. The messages must have a specific meaning so the client can recognize their loved ones' continued existence. Many clients share that having a one-hour direct line with their loved ones in spirit is better than a year of therapy!

— **Dreams:** Dream visits from our loved ones are a profound experience and a common sign because it's a more accessible avenue for them to speak to us. The veil between their world and ours is thinner when our mind is at rest. You are *not thinking* while sleeping; instead, you're tapped into your heart space, that mysterious space where your *knowing* lies, so you're naturally more receptive. A mind at rest removes barriers and limitations, making us more open to messages from the spirit realm.

Unlike a regular dream that is easily forgotten, dream visits are real, and you remember every detail. You just *know* it was them in spirit. It's so wonderful to be able to hug them once more and speak with them, telling them you love them and hearing it back. However, if you experience any fear or low vibration emotions in the dream, as I did when my mother passed, then you can know it is not a true dream visitation. Instead, it is your own grief and pain being processed through your dream.

If you haven't experienced a visitation dream yet, know that it does help to *ask* them to visit! Before falling asleep, meditate on a memory you have with them. And if it doesn't happen right away, try again the next night and the next. Remember, they are also learning to reach you and want to, more than anything. Trust the process, and don't give up.

— **Phone calls:** As incredible as it seems, you can even receive phone calls and messages from loved ones in spirit! *Out of nowhere*, just when you are thinking of your loved one, a phone call or text message comes onto your phone with their name on it. That can happen even when they have been gone for many years. It is sometimes on a very special day or before a special event. The phone may ring, and up pops their name on the screen; all you hear is silence or static upon answering it.

If this seems difficult to believe, I assure you I have witnessed it with my own eyes—and ears! Several of my clients have come to me and shown me text messages from their deceased loved one's number, even though the number was no longer in operation. In every case, the person had asked for a sign, and boom, a text with their loved one's name and number would pop up on the screen. These forms of communication are rare but, as you can imagine, *potent.*

— **Angel numbers:** Seeing repetitive numbers on our phones, clocks, or license plates is an easy way for spirits to communicate with us. These are known as angel numbers, and they usually appear in sequences such as 1212, 1111, 333, and so on. You might see the same numbers for weeks straight around the same time or place.

— **Family gatherings:** Family gatherings are a time when spirits love to be present and join in on the fun. Full of love and laughter, gatherings carry a high vibration that makes the connection easier. Allow *whatever* comes in during these high-energy moments to flow to your heart space. Don't disregard any information you receive during these times.

Missing Our Messages

Many people come into my office thinking their loved ones *don't* want to communicate with them because they haven't received a sign since passing. Once we start talking, they often realize that they have, in fact, received signs, but they didn't trust them and therefore wrote them off. Or they see that they had been blocking messages because they thought it couldn't possibly be—their limiting beliefs and the low vibration of grief were hindering any connection. Never forget that they love you and want to communicate with you.

I always liken the process of communicating with spirits to the child who pulls on his mother's pant leg, repeatedly saying, "Mommy, Mommy, Mommy!" Mommy is busy cooking, thinking about her to-do list, and not paying attention to the child. The child continues to ask her for attention, but Mommy's not responding because she is preoccupied.

Fifteen minutes later, when Mommy's no longer busy, she may ask the child what they needed or wanted to share, but as time passes, the child may not remember and says, "I forgot, and you weren't paying attention anyway." This is very similar to how our loved ones attempt to communicate with us—we are often too preoccupied with the busyness of our everyday lives to give our undivided attention.

You must make an effort to avoid giving your loved ones in spirit the impression that you may be uninterested, inattentive, too distracted, or in disbelief of their efforts to connect with you. Despite this, they will never stop *trying* to communicate. Paying close attention and trusting their messages can significantly enhance your ability to communicate with your loved ones.

If your loved ones are trying to reach you, keeping an open heart and mind will make it easier for them to communicate. Be aware of the voices inside and outside of your mind. Consider that unusual things you s*aw, felt, heard, and experienced* were real and not coincidental. Don't assume it's all a figment of your imagination. If something comes into your head, trust it instead of saying, "That is just what I think they would say; it's not really them."

It's imperative to tap into the "little brain" of your heart to speak to your loved ones, as love is the specialty of the heart, and love is the language of the spirit world. Whether we have physical bodies or not, love remains. And love wants you to be aware of itself. It wants to express itself; therefore, love will do anything it can to reach you. And it will reach you! Until then, keep healing, practicing, and paying attention. Keep moving one step at a time on the long journey toward your heart's connection to the spirits *waiting* to share their love.

IN THEIR OWN WORDS:
Karen D.

About two years ago, on my birthday, I bought one of Susan's hour-long mediumship sessions to discuss my mom, who had passed, and see if there was anything she had to tell me. Well, of course, she did; the reading was mind-boggling and incredible. I loved every second of it and took notes, and at the very end, right before we were to hang up from the Zoom call, Susan insisted that my mom would send me a balloon as a sign. A balloon seemed kind of random—and Susan even said it was odd—but that's what my mom said!

The next day, I went to Laguna Beach to celebrate my birthday with my siblings and told my sister about my reading. I read her all the notes I took during our session. She was all excited to hear it, and I was super enthusiastic, of course, because it was so mind-blowing that I was supposed to receive some kind of balloon sign.

I wasn't sure if that was ever going to happen, but when we were done at the beach and I was walking up the hill to my car, lo and behold, underneath my car was a white balloon that was hovering right near the back tire by the tailgate. I needed to open the tailgate first, so I knew my mom had put it there for me because it was placed perfectly in my sight as I walked up the hill.

As you can imagine, I just about lost my mind! I grabbed the balloon. It was a little deflated but still in good shape, and I started screaming and yelling to my sister, who was getting in her car down the street. "Look! Look! I got my balloon! Mom sent me the balloon just like she said she would. Susan was right all along!"

I took that balloon home with me, talked to it, and kept it as long as possible. Of course, it lost all its air over time, but I still have it! What an incredible memory that was! I'll never forget that last-minute sign, custom-made just for me.

IN THEIR OWN WORDS:
Melissa B.

A few years after my mother's passing, we were decorating for Christmas, and this beautiful monarch butterfly was flexing its wings on a daisy bush right in front of me and didn't move; it let me walk all the way up and take a video of it. I told my husband I knew it was my momma. Christmas was her favorite season.

After that day, butterflies would come to me on some difficult days, and I know it was her sending me her love just to let me know she was still with me. Eight years later, when I came to Susan for a reading, she said, "Your mother sends you butterflies." I was utterly blown away!

IN THEIR OWN WORDS:
Kathleen S.

A few days before the first anniversary of my husband's death, I sat for a reading by Susan. She told me my husband wanted to tell me how much he loved me and was sorry for leaving me so suddenly. She said he told her he was always around me and loved to send me birds. "This bird will act differently, not like the usual birds we see all the time. He is sending them to you to let you know he's there, beside you."

The next evening, I took a short walk around our block and heard a strange screeching noise that I couldn't identify. I thought maybe it was barking and then put it out of my mind. The next morning, when I was putting my dogs in the car to take them to the vet, I heard the same screeching noise coming down the street. I turned around to see a beautiful male peacock strolling up our street, even coming up my driveway and onto my yard.

My husband's daughter and grandson saw the bird in my front yard when they came over later to walk my dogs. He also made an appearance at my house the day I came back from a vacation, and my husband's daughter was picking me up from the airport, and her son was staying at the house.

I told Susan about the peacock's visits when I had another reading with her shortly before the second anniversary of my husband's death. She said he probably wouldn't be able to send me the peacock again within two days but to look for it within the next couple of weeks and let her know because "it would be a really big deal."

A few weeks later, I went to Hawaii on a long weekend with my friend Cathy. I was excited because I had never been to Hawaii. While we were having breakfast on our second day in Hawaii, I saw Cathy tear up when reading her phone. She told me her son was at an event her late father would have enjoyed, and he had sent her a text saying how much he missed his grandfather.

While walking back to the hotel, Cathy saw a butterfly and said, "Hi, Dad." She turned to me and said, "That's a sign from my father. He sends me butterflies in the West and cardinals in the East." Cathy knew my peacock story, and I told her I liked the hotel where we were staying, mainly because the historical pictures in the lobby included some peacocks.

Cathy and I returned to the room and were chatting about nothing important when the décor in the room suddenly stopped me in my tracks. The motif on the light blue wallpaper behind the queen beds was one of the large peacock feathers.

After giving it some thought, I think I know why my husband chose peacocks as a symbol to show he's still around. In the summer after he passed, I kept myself busy with household projects and had some new landscaping done in the backyard. I bought new patio furniture with blue cushions and several small metal peacocks for decorations. Sending me peacocks and peacock motifs is my husband's way of acknowledging me, our home, and our love.

IN THEIR OWN WORDS:
Amy & Allison

From Amy: In May 2020, we lost my best friend, my kids' dad, to suicide. It was a very uncertain and scary time for us. We decided to go to a live event with Susan one night, and she picked my daughter Allison for the first reading. She told us things only he would know and gave us signs to look for. We spoke only five minutes or less, so we decided to book an appointment with Susan to obtain more information.

During our reading, Susan didn't know much about what was happening in our life, but for some reason, she called upon my daughter Emily. Her dad used to call her "Em," and that's what Susan kept calling her. She also said that the first letter of the person we were missing began with a "J," and she thought he was saying Juan but, in fact, his name was Jon.

She also said Jon liked to mess with me by turning off the lights, and she asked if I could smell him. At first, I thought that was very strange, but it turns out that I could. He was a smoker, and I continually have smelled that smoke all around me since he passed, but nobody in my house smokes.

Without us telling her, Susan knew exactly how he died, which was crazy because that hadn't been announced anywhere. We were stunned that she knew this private information. He would always say, "I'm gonna get it together," and he said that through her in our reading numerous times.

He also said that he was in a good place and that he was happy and out of pain.

She told us to look for a crow as a sign from Jon—a solitary black crow. We now see lone black crows all the time. The other day there were hundreds of crows in the trees above our house, and we were the only house with that on our whole block. We like to think Jon shared all his "friends" in the trees to show us he is now happy.

From Allison: I took a road trip with my boyfriend to San Francisco and stopped in Carmel. We were on some rocks overlooking the ocean when we noticed a crow sitting on a rock right next to me. Whenever this happens, I know that my dad, Jon, is present because, during our reading with Susan, she told us "he shows himself by sending a crow." Having a reading with Susan helped us see the signs to look for from him, and now we see and feel him around us all the time.

INTEGRATION MOMENT
Becoming Heart Smart

We connect through soul; we join through heart. If you can get in touch with your heart space, you can get in touch with your soul and other souls you love. Overcoming limiting beliefs is key when connecting to your departed loved ones via your heart space. Remember, there are no right or wrong ways to communicate, but I invite you to choose any of the prompts below to help you achieve this goal:

- What does the term "limiting beliefs" mean to you?

- What created the limiting beliefs in your life?

- Do these beliefs serve you now?

- List some ways you can release the beliefs holding you back from allowing your departed loved ones to enter your energetic field to connect with you.

- Do you believe that souls are eternal? If not, what reasoning is behind your disbelief?

- Name some ways fear has hindered you from connecting with loved ones in the spirit world.

Chapter Exercises

Spirit communicates through our senses, including the "sixth sense," our intuition. Try these exercises to help open up the pathway of communication with your loved ones in spirit:

- Psychometry is the ability to read information through touch. It can be a powerful way to tap into your loved one's energy. It's believed that objects can hold energy and that the energy that is left behind will give you a line of communication. Hold onto an object that is meaningful to your loved ones. It is believed that their energy leaves a lasting imprint, and that imprint is now on the objects they love.

- Let them know that you're trying to communicate with them. An item can be a vine to their soul, just as your love is. Talk to them and ask them for signs. If you don't have an item from your loved one, go to a place they loved and spend time there talking to them. Memories create a link between their consciousness and yours.

- Automatic writing opens the energetic pathways, which helps exercise the part of the soul that communicates with the unseen. Tap into your heart space, which is the seat of your soul. Start the exercise by putting your hand to your heart and asking your loved ones to send you a message. Clear your mind and put your pen to paper, writing everything that comes through. You don't have to think about what to write, you don't even have to look at the paper, and you shouldn't go back and look while you're in the writing process. Just continue writing anything that comes through until nothing is left to write.

- Remember that our loved ones communicate differently through writing. While you are writing, your expectation may be that your deceased loved ones will communicate the same way they communicated when they were alive, but this isn't possible. You may hear their voice or simply know what they are trying to say. Allow the messages to come automatically.

- As you continue writing, you are releasing and letting the information move beyond your senses. Be clear in your intentions and speak from your heart prior to beginning. Ask them a few questions and then put pen to paper. Remember, allow it to flow naturally.

CHAPTER 9

Mastering Fear, Harnessing Intuition

The time I have spent in the spirit world has shown me clearly that it's a world *completely* free of fear; there is simply loving awareness. But that, of course, isn't true for the material world we inhabit as humans. The truth is this physical world, with its plethora of dangers, is alarming in many ways. All you have to do is turn on the nightly news to understand why many people naturally have their guard up while living in a state of anxiety, worry, and fear.

Despite all the potential dangers of this material world, the spirit world wants nothing more than for us to have a life driven by intuitive, loving awareness, free of the vibration of fear, right here on earth. We are meant to learn how to master our fear and harness our intuition. But how exactly do we discern the fine line between fear and intuition? Understanding the difference between the two can be, and often is, the difference between life and death—and nothing has taught me that more than my work in the field of forensic mediumship.

The field of forensic mediumship involves using one's mediumship abilities to bring forward evidential information from the spirit world to help families, private investigators, police, or other law enforcement agencies with missing person cases and other unsolved crimes. This might sound like a pretty frightening field to work in, as it's dealing head-on with some of the most broken parts of humanity. But, at the core, forensic mediumship is all about learning to *unplug* from the deafening fear that typically steers us, so that we can instead tap into the quiet, intuitive voice of the soul.

Prior to having any professional experience in the forensic mediumship field, I had a personal experience that set the stage for much of my journey into this work— and helps set the stage for this chapter.

Pre-incident Indicators

In 2007, I was attending a party thrown by good friends of mine, the Guerreros, well-known WWE wrestlers. While there, I chatted for some time with one of the guests, another famous wrestler. It was the first time I had met him, and I didn't know anything about him or his circumstances. He was there with his wife and young son, and during our chat, he disclosed that he had a *severe* and lingering back injury but needed to return to wrestling to support his family. Though I hardly knew him, I more or less suggested that he not return to wrestling anytime soon. That little intuitive voice inside me told me something terrible could happen if he returned to the ring too quickly.

During this conversation, his wife looked at me with concerned eyes, affirming what I felt in my gut. *Please listen and don't go back to work*, she seemed to be thinking. Immediately I knew this wasn't just a bad idea but a potentially deadly one. Well, if you're a WWE fan, you know that Chris Benoit did go back to work, and just a couple months after he did, he killed his wife and young child in a horrific tragedy before ending his own life.

I didn't know it then, but this was a forensic mediumship experience, despite the information coming to me *before* the crime. Situations like this are known as "pre-incident indicators" (PINS), which are events and behaviors that often precede violence. Gavin de Becker, a forensics expert, states in his book *The Gift of Fear*, "By noticing pre-incident indicators, individuals can better predict violence before it occurs and, therefore, take the necessary precautions and actions to stay safe."

This incident shook me to my core. I suddenly understood how valuable volunteering my time and skills could be in this arena. I had often focused on trying to piece together the mysteries of high-profile missing person cases at parties when I was younger and had briefly interned at the National Center for Missing & Exploited Children as a young adult. But now I was seriously interested in forensics work—to the point of understanding it was an intricate part of my life purpose. So, I dove into learning the craft of forensic mediumship and the confusing relationship between fear and intuition as best as I could.

What Is Fear?

There have been many times when a thought that something negative might happen in the future would come to the forefront of my mind; however, I often doubted the information, knowing clearly that my mind could play tricks on me. Fortunately, not all our thoughts are premonitions; some are simply rooted in fear. (It is key to remember, "What you fear, you feed!") So in this encounter with Chris Benoit, how could I know the information coming through *was* a premonition, born from intuition rather than fear? As the title of this chapter suggests, the prerequisite to harnessing our intuition is mastering our fears. To do that, we must first understand what fear is, exactly, as the line between fear and intuition can be very blurry.

There are two types of fear: real and illusory. Real fear is the kind that triggers primal responses that protect us. For instance, if an unknown person were to start chasing you down the street, you would run—and it's *real* fear that gets your feet moving. Real fear is set in the present moment and is essential for survival.

On the other hand, illusory fear is anxiety about what could go wrong rather than what is actually happening now. This brand of fear is rampantly available in our human world. Set in the "what if" of the future rather than the reality of the now, illusory fear ultimately hinders living life to the fullest if it's not overcome.

If you're like most people, you can quickly rattle off a list of things you fear, and chances are most, if not all, of those fears are illusory. It is for this reason that sages from time immemorial have advised us to face our fears to neutralize them. Once we master our illusory fears, it clears the way to live a Spirit-led life guided by our intuition, which is what Spirit wants for us—the secret to life, indeed! As philosopher Ralph Waldo Emerson said, "He who is not every day conquering some fear has not learned the secret of life."

Illusory fear and intuitive hits are future-focused and, therefore, easily confused. While we tend to internalize our illusory fears as real, we similarly tend to belittle our intuitive voices. The spirit world is always sending us signs of validation and caution; the problem is we often write these off as "coincidence" or "paranoia." That's why understanding the difference between illusory fear and intuition is vital for living a Spirit-led life in a sometimes-frightening world.

So, what's the trick to discerning whether it's fear or intuition? It starts with examining the feelings in your gut. Feel anxious and overwhelmed? That's fear. Feel calm and certain? That's intuition.

Our intuitive voice comes to us as a neutral thought. While the message could be scary (for example, *this person is not safe*), the way it arrives is calm and factual. It is not necessarily calming information, but it's peaceful in *feeling* when it's delivered. In other words, it isn't a story that your anxious, fear-based mind created and is obsessed with, but a message from your soul meant to guide or protect you or someone else.

Intuition is a sudden knowing, an instant understanding of something you otherwise wouldn't have considered. Intuition is *affirming.* Fear, on the other hand, can be a very dark, heavy, or terrifying energy.

When we are steeped in illusory fear, we are constantly on high alert; when we are in sync with our intuition, we are in a state of affirmative awareness. In other words, while illusory fear is messy, intuition is straightforward. Real fear keeps us safe; intuition keeps us safe—but illusory fear does not.

Mastering illusory fear really just comes down to a simple reality check: Ask yourself, *is this real or imagined fear?* If it's real, run, so to speak. If it's imagined, shift gears; turn the volume way down on that irrational "what if" voice for a moment so that you can better hear what your calm, intuitive voice has to say.

Beginning Forensic Mediumship

As I began to place more emphasis on learning forensic mediumship alongside my regular practice, I organically became more proficient at questioning my senses to be sure my intuition was not, in fact, fear. I could better sense when it was actually coming from that place in my gut, that knowing place, that tells me something significant needs to be addressed. I began taking advanced forensic mediumship courses with many notable teachers, including Tony Stockwell from Arthur Findlay College. In his class, Tony used real forensic pictures to train us. As he called on us to figure out what had happened to the people in the pictures, I ended up realizing how spot-on I was with this kind of work—and how passionate about it too. To this day, I still use this picture method when teaching my own forensic courses because I find it so powerful.

Shortly after I finished these advanced courses, an unfortunate event arose that required my skill set. A fellow medium and previous teacher of mine asked for my help on a missing person case she was working on involving a woman, "Laura," who had Alzheimer's. Laura had been camping with her husband and disappeared while he was showering in the RV. For two long days, the information was just not coming to me. I was devastated that I couldn't tap into where Laura was, no matter how hard I pushed. On the third day, I sat at my computer, and it all poured out.

I suddenly knew Laura was still in close proximity to the camp and which direction to search in. I knew she was wearing white cutoff pants and white shoes. I knew she had left the camp and was walking around looking for coffee when she realized a cougar was shadowing her. I knew as she tried to get away from the cat, she fell off a small cliff into dense brush and hit her head. I wrote down everything and sent it to my colleague.

When I first communicated with Laura's spirit, she shared what had happened to her, and I saw that she was no longer conscious in this physical world. She told me that she would be found on a Wednesday within a couple of months by a utility worker on a maintenance call. This information was forwarded to all involved as I remained an anonymous source, but the detective said it was all "impossible," stressing that if she were as close to the camp as I said, the search dogs would have found her.

I was so invested in this case and attached to the spirit of Laura, but eventually I had to consciously release it, knowing I had done my part. I'd relayed the messages to the best of my ability, and there was nothing more I could do about whether the information would be taken seriously or not. Laura was the mother of a public figure, so the case was highly publicized, but I had to stop following it for my well-being. My colleague told me they were searching elsewhere for her than in the direction I had given them. At this point, I had to let go completely.

I received an e-mail some months later, relaying that Laura was found less than a mile from the camp, on a Wednesday, just as Laura shared. She was found by a worker, who spotted her by her white pants and white shoes poking out of the dense brush. My colleague highly encouraged me to continue doing this work. She felt the impact this work could have on families of the missing carried such importance that I had to consider moving forward in utilizing this skill.

While I wanted to pursue this kind of work, at this point it became apparent that my discernment of intuition versus illusory fear needed more mastering. I continued to study to capture a clearer understanding of all that would be required and kept helping on cases with teachers and specialized forensic mediums.

Despite the fear inherent to this line of work, I continued learning more as I entered more classes. As calls from family members and detectives began coming in to request my help, my skill level and my confidence increased. I was now on my way to helping many grieving families receive closure. I overcame my own fears and increasingly began to trust my intuition, which allowed me to help others trust themselves and master a clear sense of their surroundings.

Another profound forensics case I worked on called my own illusory fear into question. It involved a missing U.S. Army captain, "Justine." Justine and her dog disappeared when going out to meet some friends, and her boyfriend, "Jack," called me, hoping I could assist with the criminal investigation. As he told me what they knew, which was very little, I saw that Justine and her dog had left this earth. I did not relay that information outright, as previous experiences had taught me to keep that type of message to myself. "Let me try to locate her," I said.

Justine showed me that a man named Jack was her murderer and that she had married and then divorced him due to his acts of violence toward her. Here's where my fear enters the scene, muddying things up: I panicked because the man calling me was named Jack! He referred to himself as her boyfriend, not her husband, so I was confused. (Again, fear is messy.)

My fear involved my reaction to the information Justine provided, and I forgot to call upon my intuition to find calm and see things clearer. Trying not to show my fear of potentially speaking on the phone with a murderer, I asked Jack if he was married to Justine. He said no but her ex-husband's name was also Jack. Although that was a relief, I still felt some fear. I needed to tap into truth by distinguishing between fear and intuition.

With that critical detail figured out, I knew that Jack, the ex-husband, had killed her. I could hear all his ideas about how to get rid of the bodies of her and her dog as if they were my own. After removing the evidence, he drove her car into the mountains and down a hill several blocks from her house to make it seem like she was taken close to home. He left her keys and purse in the car to make it look as though she was taken out of her vehicle by force. He then headed back to his home in Arizona. Justine asked me to tell her loved ones that the police would be able to find much of the evidence they needed in the car and through surveillance cameras from homes in the surrounding area. She said that once arrested, Jack would lead police to her body to avoid the death penalty, and that's precisely how it all came to pass.

Through trial and error, I have found working with loved ones of the missing is one of my areas of expertise. I work on a few cases a year and that is enough for me now. It is very trying on your heart to see the pain and confusion in the families living through these tragic events.

Trust Your Gut

Have you ever been waiting for a driver, and when the car finally reaches you, the door opens to reveal someone who instantly gives you an uncomfortable feeling in your gut? It could be the most clean-cut person, flashing the biggest smile, with no glaringly obvious physical or behavioral indicators of any ill will, but for whatever reason, your gut whispers to you: *don't get in that car!* If you're like most people, you'll ignore that small (but mighty) intuitive voice and get in anyway. And it's precisely in situations like this, when people talk themselves out of their inner knowing, that some of the most tragic scenarios unfold, such as kidnappings, violence, and murder.

It's rare that people listen to that gut instinct and wait for another car. Why is this? Because we place more value on social cohesion, wanting to be kind, and blending in; therefore, we don't honor our intuition. However, it's when we begin to honor those natural instincts that we become spiritually connected people who understand self-protection.

A great example of this is with one of my clients, who I'll call Nicole, who narrowly escaped probable murder because she *did* listen to that voice screaming inside her. She was on a second date with a man she'd met on a dating app. The first date had gone well, and they had established some semblance of trust, so she decided to let him drive her to their destination. During the drive that night, her date suddenly said he had to pull over for a second to get something from the back of his truck. Feeling a bit strange about that, she tried to watch what he was doing through the side-view mirror and caught a glimpse of a shovel, some rope, and a blanket in the back.

You have to go NOW, her gut told her. Her mind fought back: *Maybe he's just a hunter? Maybe he just worked construction on the side? Maybe he's just a very handy man?* All these things could have been used to explain away her intuitive hit, but she chose to listen to it. She got out of the car and told him she felt suddenly unwell and needed to go home, leaving him confused.

Nicole called me a few days later to check whether this guy really was a bad person or if she was just paranoid. I affirmed her intuitive nudges and told her that his energy felt very dangerous to me. I also shared that I didn't know if he was a killer, but I knew he was definitely connected to one. Soon after that, she discovered that he was the brother of a serial killer who had recently been arrested and charged in California.

What would have happened if she didn't get out of the car? Maybe nothing, but my gut says otherwise, and so did hers. And that is *all* that matters. The point is that she trusted her instincts enough to get out of the car, not only because she saw some questionable items but more importantly because she felt deep in her bones that something was off. Please remember that when something *feels* off, the chances are high that it *is*.

This entire chapter is about the vital importance of distinguishing between fear and intuition so that you and the people you love remain as safe as possible in an unpredictable world. The irony is that people who live their lives steeped in illusory fear really want to stay safe, but their allegiance to fear actually places them in harm's way on many levels. It's our intuition that keeps us safe, and that's the muscle we must strengthen.

Our inner intuitive voice truly is the voice of Spirit, and Spirit wants nothing but to help us. It's our job to remember that strengthening trust in Spirit is the pathway to strengthening our clear connection to our intuitive self, and in doing so, lends to a safer environment for ourselves and those we love.

Some of my intuitive abilities came from forensics and my experiences while on the other side. Although I didn't fully understand as a child and spent years not acknowledging my own personal power of intuition, I saw spirits consistently communicating with intuition and telepathy.

I *felt* the power and knowledge of the spirits and how they seemed to just *know* things without thought. Unlike humans, they don't have to rely on the trust of self due to the fact that intuition and telepathy are natural forms of spirit communication. They don't have to ask someone, "Are you sad?"—they just *know*.

Our souls are cut from the same cloth; therefore, we have the natural ability to tap into our own intuitive understanding. Intuition isn't foreign to our soul; in actuality, it is part of our inherent skill set, just like the souls on the other side. We only need to learn how to integrate our spirit consciousness with our soul, which creates a clearer understanding of the spirit world, which in turn creates inner peace and connection.

A personal example of using my own intuition (and releasing fear in the process) was when my daughter was pregnant. I was awoken by a small voice telling me the baby couldn't breathe. I sat up in my bed and asked for confirmation of the information I heard, making sure it wasn't merely my own fear. I heard, "Nana, I cannot breathe."

The announcement was frightening, but it came to me calmly, so I knew in my gut it was important. Half asleep, I arose from bed and heard again that something was blocking the baby's breathing and that I should get something bubbly to drink for my daughter. Trusting that intuitive voice, I did just that.

When I woke my daughter, I quietly asked her if she could feel the baby. She jiggled and wiggled, but to her shock, the baby wasn't moving. Naturally, she panicked. I calmly sat her up and gave her the drink I had been instructed to gather. She swallowed it, and the baby started moving again! I was told then that my daughter and the baby would be okay for that evening but to take her to the hospital the next morning to see if she had a true knot.

At the hospital the next day, my daughter was induced—within just 12 hours of that spirit communication. My granddaughter is here today because I listened to that inner voice that is always speaking to us, just as *I* am here today because my mother listened to her intuition when she heard it whisper years ago, "Your baby is in the freezer."

The Five Phases of Harnessing Your Intuition

Intuition is a powerful source that everyone should learn to master in order to better their lives. Here are my five phases to harnessing your intuition—which stage are you in?

PHASE 1:
What Is This Feeling?

In this initial phase, your intuition seems to be random and inconsistent, like it just comes out of the blue. You feel *something*, but you don't know what it is. You feel unsure, as if your imagination is running away with you. You easily confuse intuition with fear.

In this stage:

- You question if your intuition or gut feelings are accurate.

- You may not even be aware of what you are experiencing, but you know it feels different, almost like an "ah-ha" moment.

- You feel a slight nudge to listen to that feeling inside, but you feel primarily unsure.

- You continue to wonder, is this real or am I making it up?

This is a perfect place to start, where curiosity pulls you to know more. You want to understand this feeling that keeps coming up without fear or confusion. You are right where you need to be to begin the process of harnessing your natural intuition.

PHASE 2:
It's Becoming a Familiar Feeling

In this phase, you realize intuition feels different from fear. It creates a gut feeling, as this is where intuition sits— in your gut! It will come and go, but you are beginning to feel the familiarity of this feeling. You do not yet understand the difference between your thinking mind and intuitive sense.

In this stage:

- You begin to recognize the feeling as something different than fear or imagination.

- You cannot yet distinguish between fear and intuition, but you are beginning that process.

- You need to be more aware and understand your intuition, and you are beginning to pay closer attention to it when it comes into your gut.

You are beginning to understand in more depth, that it can be helpful to listen to feelings instead of just logical thinking. You want more understanding of this newfound experience of intuition.

PHASE 3:

Discovery—You Begin Tapping into Your Intuition

In this phase, the goal is to develop a consistent and trustworthy notation of the feelings coming from your intuition. You begin to practice using techniques to arouse that intuitive understanding. You are now working on the discovery phase. It is real, you feel it, and you want to know more about it. You realize the more you acknowledge it, the clearer it is, and the more in control you feel.

In this stage:

- You begin to tap into that intuitive feeling on your own.

- You should practice in situations that do not carry danger but simply guide you to that gut source.

- You are now beginning to use it, trust it, and your practice is starting to show results.

- It's time to practice, practice, and practice more.

You are ready to learn the contrast of the feelings. One way to do this is to ask yourself what you feel in your gut before entering a room or being in an unfamiliar environment. Be consistent and begin to work on feeling the difference between correct intuitive information and incorrect information. Remember that being incorrect teaches you how to be correct as you begin to acknowledge the difference between the two feelings ahead of time.

PHASE 4:
Release Fear and Trust the Process

In this phase, your intuition is becoming more evident, yet you still fear being wrong. It is time to release the fear of right or wrong and simply trust. Start small, and when you know it's starting to work, and you see the accuracy, your fears will begin to fade.

In this stage:

- Things are beginning to come together; therefore, you trust your intuition more than you had before.

- You are now using your intuition more often, which helps you see it can make sense and creates a favorable outcome.

- You are starting your day with intuitive feelings instead of from the headspace of fear.

- This is no longer overwhelming, and the trust level is improving. Now it is a matter of allowing it to flow.

PHASE 5:
Let Go and Allow

In this phase, you are now unconsciously letting go of the fear baseline and allowing the intuitive information to come as it deems necessary. You allow it to flow and now feel the superpower of trusting your intuitive knowledge. Not always, because fear will always try to step in, but you are learning to effectively push it aside and return to that peaceful state of intuition.

In this stage:

- You are now receiving more reliable information, which feels empowering.

- You no longer push away intuitive information; therefore, you feel more in control of your choices and surroundings.

- You fully trust your intuition and know it is always there to help you.

- You continue to release the fears that arise and step into your power at any given moment.

- You are now letting go and allowing the intuitive information to flow and serve your highest good.

Remember, you will always be working on exploring your intuition, as it is a constant challenge to trust your gut instead of your fear. Be gentle with yourself and know that as you work with your intuition, so it will work with you.

❀ ❀ ❀

The stories in this chapter are just the tip of the iceberg regarding what I've learned about fear and intuition from my forays into forensic mediumship. Still, I hope they will serve as valuable examples in understanding the vital difference between the two.

Does listening to your intuition mean that you can always prevent a harmful event from occurring? No! Can it help? Yes! And practice is your friend in learning to use these tools out in the world. When you learn to master imaginary fear and then tap into and recognize legitimate warning signs via intuitive gut hits, avoiding unfavorable circumstances in your life *without* living in the constant vibration of fear becomes possible.

My forensic work taught me how to view the outside world differently and always be aware of my surroundings and intuition so that I'm not stepping into fear; therefore, I am vigilant in recognizing and avoiding potential opportunities for crime or harm in my environment. Navigating your life by intuition's compass could potentially save your life one day; God forbid you ever find yourself in possible danger.

Looking back on my life, it makes perfect sense that I am so connected to forensic mediumship work. Considering my past as a sexual abuse survivor for much of my younger years, both fear and intuition became my best friends. I believe that offering my mediumship abilities to help others later in life was an inevitable part of my soul contract. Why did I go through years of abuse at the hands of perpetrators? I might never know the complete answer to that question. Still, I do know that it resulted in my wanting to do everything in my power to transmute those painful experiences into a way to help others, and forensic mediumship was one of the many avenues for me to do just that.

INTEGRATION MOMENT
Getting in Touch with Your Gut

While "forensics" is all about logic and fact, "mediumship" relies entirely on intuition. The two polarities rub against one another in forensic mediumship, but that is what makes it great. The same dichotomy is true for your life and, just like in the world of forensics, finding the balance between the two is the key to ultimate success. However, when a society prizes the logical mind above all, it becomes challenging to take the road less traveled. Learn to lean in to your gut feelings and develop spirit consciousness through practicing trust between Spirit and yourself. Explore your relationship with this balance with any of the following journal prompts:

- In what ways do you navigate your life and experiences from imagined fear?

- How could you better use your intuition to be self-protective?

- Name a few times in your life when something seemingly bad was going to happen or something happened that triggered you into fear.

- What actions did you take to handle those incidents?

- What could you have done differently, if anything?

- How do you distinguish between fear-based thinking and intuition?

- When have you been in a situation where you haven't acknowledged the lack of safety, but you felt something and stifled it, and then something happened?

- What is your relationship with fear?

- What is your relationship with intuition?

- Do you feel balanced or unbalanced? Explain.

- If unbalanced, what changes could you make to reach a better balance in your life?

- When have you been in situations where you didn't listen to your gut, and something happened that may have been avoided by having trusted or listened to your instincts?

Chapter Exercises

How many times have your instincts said to you, "Don't go to that party" or "Don't trust that person behind you," among many other warnings? How often do you ignore it, only to have something negative happen that may have been avoided? Our intuition is so strong that it can even tell us when someone isn't healthy for us. Of course, most people don't walk away; instead, they start a relationship only to say later, "I knew it; why didn't I listen to my gut?!" We often tell ourselves, "Maybe I am just being silly; maybe this is just my fear taking over." That could be accurate under some circumstances, but we won't know when we are correct about people, places, things, and situations if we don't listen and learn about harnessing our own personal intuition. Fear can be our friend; however, learning to tap into our intuition will offer us the larger picture.

Let's try a few exercises to help us begin to trust our natural-born intuition so that it is sure to be working in our favor:

- List the times you "heard the message" in your gut but didn't follow what you knew to be correct. What was the outcome of those situations?

- List all the times you heard the message in your gut, and you trusted that message. What was the outcome?

- After practicing the Five Phases of Harnessing Your Intuition, think about how it has helped you expand your intuitive knowledge and offered you the opportunity to do things differently.

- Write the different ways in which fear has controlled your choices. What would have been different if you didn't allow fear to dictate those choices?

- Now that you understand the difference between fear and intuition, practice this Spirit-given gift in all your interactions.

Feel the empowerment of your own process when learning to trust your intuition over your fear. Celebrate this achievement. Remember, you won't do this perfectly, but it will improve as you tap into your gut instinct. Don't be afraid to be wrong. Being wrong will teach you what that feels like, and you will begin to use that knowledge to pause and wait for the "right feelings" to come in. Once you understand how to use your intuition, you will be ready to handle situations that previously baffled you. You've got this!

CHAPTER 10

Healing from Grief

I'll never forget the day I was walking through my neighborhood grocery store, as I had done countless times before, and there it was waiting for me in the canned food aisle: the insurmountable mountain of grief. I was staring at a can of beans when it hit me like a bomb detonating out of nowhere, and I sobbed. You would have thought I was literally staring at the lifeless body of my recently deceased mother. I was uncontrollable—I could not control my tears, pain, and desperate longing for her. And that's how grief works: completely unpredictable, sneaking up on you when you least expect it, whenever it wants to.

As you can imagine, breaking down like that in public felt downright humiliating, not to mention isolating, as clearly no one else was feeling what I felt. I was the "abnormal" one. It seemed everyone else went on with life as usual—living, laughing, and loving as if nothing had happened—while my life had just been flipped upside down and inside out. Shattered in one fell swoop.

Grief is a monster in and of itself. I have lost many people I dearly loved during my life journey. There is no easier, softer way to say it: grief is by far the most painful emotion a person can feel. It can shake your self-esteem, your trust in your environment, the world, and even your trust in God. Grief holds all the cards; it has all the control. Grief isn't something you get to decide to be done with and walk away from; *it* decides when it is going to come make a housecall. When loss has knocked on your door, it feels as if you are defenseless, and it feels like an animal ready to pounce at any given moment. *It* has the power, *it* has the control, *it* has the trajectory, and no part of you is immune to it.

The physical death of someone we deeply love is one of the worst experiences, if not *the* worst experience, we can endure as humans. Yet, when we rewind to the lesson I learned during my afterlife journey—that life's challenges are catalysts for soul growth—grief then becomes one of the most potent invitations available to us to embark on our highest spiritual path. When seen through a spiritual lens, grief becomes a rite of passage that exists to develop the soul. An initiation. A gift—though it certainly feels the opposite at the time. As 18th-century poet William Cowper said, "Grief is itself a medicine." Of course, as with all true healing, we must first break the fever. We must first suffer the pain.

The "dark night of the soul" has been described as far back as the 16th century by the poet and mystic St. John of the Cross. Modern spiritual teacher Caroline Myss describes it in her book *Defy Gravity* as, ". . . a journey into light, a journey from your darkness into the strength and hidden resources of your soul." It is a harsh but necessary period of personal development that we experience in life that, in the end, shows us the light. It is a pruning back of all that no longer matters to awaken something deeper inside of us, resulting in a more spiritually aligned and meaningful life. The journey through dark night of the soul is a catalyst for change. A shedding. A rebirth. All that you believed and thought you were and the meaning you had previously given your life collapses with deep grief. You are forced to discover a new, more profound purpose. It's an invitation to feel the presence of your soul, your spirit, once again—to remember that you are a spiritual being having a human experience, not the other way around. Grief, it turns out, is the greatest propellant for this grueling-but-so-rewarding journey from dark to light.

The Cycle of Life and Grief

What is happening? Where am I? Where are you? How can I possibly survive this without you—do I even want *to?* Welcome to the confused, anxious mind space that is grief. Welcome to the club *no one* wants to be a part of, but so many of us are. Welcome to the pitch black. Without your consent or knowledge, grief feels as if someone has physically moved you from the comfortable, sunlit, familiar room you've long known into utterly foreign territory—a room that's dark, cold, lonely, and shrinking by the minute. You don't know *this* room, and you don't want to. It's unfamiliar, or so it feels. But the deeper truth is that you have actually been continuously grieving since the very day you were born.

We truly do live in the circle of life. Every beginning is an end, and every end a beginning. Traveling through the river (which I experienced in the Waiting Station) and settling into the water in our mother's womb is the start of our human journey. It also means we'll leave our perfect life in the spirit world. Then as soon as we think we're snug and safe in our mother's tummy, it's time, lo and behold, to leave again.

Childbirth isn't meant to be easy; babies don't want change any more than we adults do. They have a comfy cushy home they're snuggled into, and *then* the pushing begins. They become overwhelmed, their world in upheaval. They open their eyes as they are being propelled into the light, but it's a different kind of light. Strangers are touching them, and they are feeling sensations they've never experienced. They don't recall *ever* being here. It's totally unfamiliar—and they cry, feeling shocked and confused.

However, once a loving parent takes them in their arms, everything changes. They're reunited; the child feels peace and comfort in their loving embrace. That warmth, that beautiful love, is a source of comfort that relieves the stress and the fears and leaves behind any confusion that might remain. It's as if they're returning to a place of safety, and even though this is a new world, they feel secure, loved, and whole. This loving embrace is their *touchstone* as they learn and grow. They will always carry the love of that moment when they were first held, and they felt the warmth, peace, and safety only love can provide.

(For clarity, I would like to address the special bond an adoptive parent has with their baby. As an adoptive mother myself, I know firsthand the moment I held my babies in my arms, that same mystical, magical oneness, that security, was there. We were *reunited in soul* and we were *together at last*. That moment, that ever so precious moment, remains with me until this day. A parent's love knows no bounds.)

In our human journey, grief in various forms continues to be a part of our process. When our mommy takes away the blanket or milk—grief; when we have to learn to give up our diapers—grief; when we have to leave our mommy's side to go away to school for the first time—grief. These "little" moments of despair ultimately prepare us for the most intensive grief, the physical loss of someone we love. Some changes naturally bring forth grief, and the only constant in life is change; therefore, we are constantly processing through grief. One could say that life carries with it a continuous rhythm of loss. Love, joy, and grief are constantly cycling through our life experience.

Birthing and dying are incredibly similar processes. Just as birth in this world is leaving another, death in this world is also birth into another. We fight dying just as we fight being born. In both cases, we're frightened of the unknown and therefore resist. We "hold on" as long as we can because we are afraid of what we do not know. When we are in the transitioning process, we don't know what is coming, we don't know what to expect, and we don't know what awaits us on the other side. Until the time finally comes when we do know—and at that time we will know, undoubtedly, that we are safe and can finally release our fears and celebrate our return home. Once there, we immediately see our loved ones and angels, hear the most beautiful music, and feel an overwhelming sense of peace and unconditional love. *Ahhh, we can breathe, we are home again!*

The problem is that the loved ones we left behind on the human plane *don't* know we are safe. They, instead, are riddled with grief and plagued with thoughts of where we have gone and if they will ever see us again. The bereaved aren't afforded peace because they don't know that their loved ones on the other side are happy, healthy, and still very much alive and present. That is why direct knowledge of the afterlife, of our soul's eternal existence, is essential to soothing our grief.

Navigating through Grief

When we understand that grief is a normal part of our life journey and that it is actually helpful to our soul's growth, we can start to look at ways to navigate *through* the grief rather than *drowning* in it. Historically, nearly all societies, no matter where in the world, had a consistent structure for the grieving process, and they were all centered around community. Grieving together in public was deemed essential. Healthy. However, with the decline of religion and faith-based communities in the modern world, many in our current culture do not have a structure for grief, and so many must go it alone. Like most everything else in the Western world, the mourning process has become privatized. That is unfortunate because just as raising a child takes a village, so does effectively processing the loss of a loved one. Without a community to share the burden of grief with, we have nowhere to turn to process it, forcing us to turn inward alone.

So, let's look at grief head-on, right now, together.

The five stages of grief were introduced by Elisabeth Kübler-Ross in her 1969 book *On Death and Dying*: denial, anger, bargaining, depression, and acceptance. While this model is a helpful navigational tool, please keep in mind that the grief process, no matter how many tools we have, is *messy*. It's good that we attempt to map out the terrain of unfamiliar territory. Still, the ultimate truth of grief is that it is far from predictable or logical. It's a wilderness, each and every time we encounter it.

Grief generally means experiencing a period of deep sorrow, numbness, and even guilt and anger, with these feelings gradually easing over time. But not every grief is the same because not every death is the same. Not every love is the same. There is no "typical" way to grieve, just as there are no "average" timelines in healing. Though some common physical and psychological experiences fall under the umbrella of grief—insomnia, emotional numbness, social withdrawal, loss of appetite, hopelessness, guilt, and so on—actual grief of losing a loved one is an entirely individualized experience, unique to each person who is experiencing the loss.

The passing of your neighbor won't touch the pain of losing your child, God forbid. Losing your mother suddenly at a young age will feel much different than her passing from a long illness at the age of 90. Both are equally painful; however, one appears more tragic. And if someone you love chooses to end their own life, this opens a whole other can of heart-wrenching pain. No matter the specific circumstance, how you deal with or don't deal with the grief will heavily affect the efficacy of your healing process.

Unexpected grief is correlated with sudden death, such as that from a heart attack, car crash, overdose, or murder. Whatever the specific circumstance, sudden grief feels like a piercing jolt to your soul that drains all your energy from you. This kind of grief hits so hard and fast that you can't take it all in—many people will drop to the floor, unable to hold themselves up. All their energy has left them. It feels as if God has just shaken you to the point that your soul can't go on any longer. It's too much. You feel this disaster that no one understands. You feel helpless and angry. *Why did it happen? How could God let this happen? Why is no one else affected by this like I am?*

Mad at the world, angry at God, you feel an intense anger that is different from other kinds of grief. With sudden grief, you also obsess over every hurtful or painful time you've had with your loved one. I found myself doing this when one of my brothers passed away suddenly. Not long before he died, he used my washer and dryer to do laundry. I was annoyed and confronted him harshly for not putting my clothes in the dryer after he had finished. After he passed, I obsessed over and over about that incident as if that were the only interaction we ever had in life! The worst part about sudden grief is that it leaves us with no chance to say good-bye, apologize, make amends, or say "I love you" one last time.

While unexpected grief is a sudden hit to your soul, **anticipatory grief**, on the other hand, is grief on a low simmer. You begin grieving before the person you love dies, which can be a confusing state to be in. It is most often associated with long-term illnesses, so I also refer to it as "illness grief."

When my father was slowly dying from a terminal illness, my grief began long before his actual death. You gradually somewhat prepare for the reality of the loss. For some, it can mean time to make amends, say good-bye, and receive a sense of closure, and this is a gift compared to sudden loss. But anticipatory grief comes with its own complex challenges. When the process goes on for a lengthy period of time, it can wear you down physically and emotionally, chipping away at you day after day until you don't even recognize yourself.

In addition, you may experience conflicting emotions when a loved one is terminally ill. On the one hand, you don't want them to pass away. On the other hand, you may hope for them to pass quickly to relieve their unbearable physical pain and your complete exhaustion. These conflicting emotions can create a sense of guilt and inner turmoil. However you experience it, grief is a beast, even if you have time to prepare and say your good-byes.

And then there's the particularly confusing and painful **grief of suicide**—a pain I personally know all too well, having lost three immediate family members and two other close friends to suicide. All suffering is dark, but I can attest that suicide is a whole different kind of dark. It's so dark that it dims something, sometimes permanently, inside us. Why? Because it feels like the ultimate rejection of love and the deepest of betrayals. When someone you love deeply would choose to leave you, it drives you to the deepest, darkest recesses of your mind. It is so difficult to accept a purposeful death, and the healing it requires is all-consuming.

When I first started sharing my story of losing two brothers, a mother, a best friend, and another person I cared deeply about to suicide, I could feel people's reactions. I felt compassion, judgment, blame, and fear in their eyes. They seemed scared to be around me, as if the possibility of suicide could somehow rub off on them or their loved ones. When someone ends their own life, they *chose* to leave you in the most permanent way—seemingly rejecting you, your love, and their time with you. And in our highly judgmental world, the shame is enough to make you want to hide away forever. Death and grief are challenging enough for people to address sincerely, but living with the stigma of suicide is a whole other beast.

The loss of my big brothers, Terry and Tommy, was gut-wrenching for me. They died by suicide three years apart, Terry when I was 27 and Tommy when I was 30. Losing one brother that way was torture; two so close together was unbearable. It felt like an awful nightmare that I couldn't wake up from. Not just any nightmare but the kind that makes you feel like you are about to implode into rubble. I couldn't feel, yet I felt it all. I was numb, yet

I felt every single cell in my body aching and withering in pain. How could it be true? I was just finally feeling like I could breathe after Terry went, and then it happened again. How do I turn back time just long enough to tell them that I need them and that I can't fathom my whole life without them here as my big brothers, as my protectors? And now, how do I protect Tommy's children from the horror and guilt I felt about not being able to keep their daddy here? How, just how?!

I could not make sense of it. I felt broken and damaged everywhere I went. I could hear people's thoughts in my head, *What kind of family did she come from that both of her brothers killed themselves? How could she not know the second time?* Wait, no, those were not other people's thoughts— those were my own! I wanted to live, and I wanted to die. There was nothing I could do to change the reality of these incomprehensible losses, this particular horror of suicide.

On a mediumship level, my brother Terry's spirit came to me three times before I found out he had killed himself, but I didn't understand that he was already dead. His soul tried to get me to listen to him while standing next to my bed calling my name, but I refused to hear him and told him to go away. For three nights, he came and went when I told him to. Then on the morning of the fourth day, I received the call that he had been found shot! He committed this ultimate atrocity of pain on my birthday. That night, while I lay in my bed, he communicated to me from the other side that the timing was not done as a punishment but as an act of love—he wanted to make sure I never forgot him.

There are no words to describe that initial feeling except that I felt a piece of me leaving, just like I felt later when Tommy died and then, still later in my life, my mother. It was shocking and sad when it was my friend who died by suicide years before my brothers, yet I was once removed, so it didn't come close to the intensity of pain I felt losing people I had loved since birth. Suicide is always terrible and inconceivable, but when it strikes your core, your immediate family, it is life shattering.

The most difficult part was having to tell my mother that her babies were gone and watch that visceral pain envelop her, not once but twice. In part, I believe that is why she chose suicide as well many years later—the pain of losing two children to suicide was unbearable for her. I would never wish this particular grief upon anyone, and I am grateful for the years I have worked to heal my pain. You see, as I have said previously, I have learned time doesn't heal us; it's what we do with the time that makes for true healing.

Additionally, people, myself included, who survive a loved one's death by suicide are plagued with the thought, *How did I not know? I should have known.* Please hear me when I say that you absolutely could not have known. I've spent many years beating myself up with this thought, but I know now that it's not healthy or accurate. The fact is that "you can't know what you don't know." I absolutely could *not* have known that my brothers and mother were going to kill themselves—it's impossible—even if I was afraid or thought it could happen, I still could not have *really* known. To conceptualize such a horror isn't possible when you love someone. It is simply unimaginable no matter what you "think" you know. It's not real until it is! I found it essential to work toward releasing the trauma and guilt plaguing my heart.

The world is often a painful place; that is a fact. And people who die by suicide are not bad or selfish; they merely want to end their intense pain. But the truth is, as every survivor of a loved one who has died by suicide knows, the pain doesn't stop with suicide—it is just transferred to those who survive the loss. With suicide grief, so much else is going on internally, and on top of the "regular" and intensely painful grief feelings, suicide grief can become unbearable. It is not uncommon for people left behind by suicide to feel suicidal themselves. It's a very normal feeling to want to *be with* the person you have lost. Sometimes, particularly in the cases of parents who lose their children to suicide, you are afraid that they still need your protection.

But I want to assure you here that all your loved ones are safe and happy, and they want nothing more than for you to continue living your life. There is no punishment on the other side for suicide; however, the ones who have chosen it do regret doing it because, with the clarity they receive on the other side, they can now see that even though human life is often painful, our soul *wants* to be here in order to grow.

Whatever type of grief you relate to, as stated, grief is a wilderness full of sorrow. It is a descent into the Dark Night of the Soul. And the worst part about it? It's incredibly lonely. With community mourning structures highly absent in today's world and a growing trend to "stay strong"—aka, avoid our feelings as much as possible— many people today do not actually go *through* the grieving process at all. Instead, they attempt to go *around* it.

Rather than facing the terrible pain of grief and dealing with loss in a healthy way, we often run from it through various numbing mechanisms, resulting in remaining stuck in a cycle of what is known as **complicated grief**. Complicated grief refers to feelings of loss that are so potent they become debilitating to one's life. The Mayo

Clinic says, "In complicated grief, painful emotions are so long-lasting and severe that you have trouble recovering from the loss and resuming your own life. . . . Complicated grief is like being in a constant, heightened state of mourning, and it keeps us from healing."* It's as if someone has turned on the spin cycle of the washing machine, and it's us in that machine, constantly spinning in blackness. From my experience, with the onset of grief, most grievers find themselves in this seemingly never-ending black hole—lost, confused, and alone.

Healing from Grief

If there's anything important enough to keep repeating, it's this: the intensity of grief decides when it's done with you, not the other way around. Still, it's important to stress that you have the choice to take an active role in your healing. I encourage you to be proactive because that is ultimately what your soul wants. If that feels impossible right now, that's okay. Like any grueling journey, it's all about taking one step at a time—even if it's a tiny baby step. Let's touch on a few helpful approaches that can assist you in taking those first steps onto the path of healing from grief.

— **Lean on others:** This is first because it is the most important. Grief leaves many people isolated, and our society prizes independence over interdependence. Finding ways to lean on others during your grieving process is vital to your healing. Whether with a grief-informed therapist, a grief support group, friends and family who have personal experience with grief, or all of the above,

---

*"Complicated Grief," Mayo Clinic, accessed October 7, 2023, https://www.mayoclinic.org/diseases-conditions/complicated-grief/symptoms-causes/syc-20360374.

talking (and talking some more!) about your debilitating feelings of loss is key to overcoming the worst of it. Do whatever you can to talk about your loved one and the despair you are feeling at the physical loss of them with other humans, even if it is difficult. *Especially* if it is difficult! As poet Henry Wadsworth Longfellow said, "There is no grief like the grief that does not speak."

— **Meditate:** The practice of meditation helps bring us into the present moment, and that is precisely where grief resides. Sometimes we must distract ourselves from that present moment on the grief journey as it would be too much to bear. But, on the flip side, constant avoidance of the pain only prolongs the healing journey. Sometimes we have to look at grief or risk being hindered by long-term, complicated grief. Meditation allows us to be in the now and address grief head-on, at least for a small part of each day. Think of it as short-term pain, long-term gain on the grief recovery path.

— **Move your body:** There are mounds of research that show grief manifests in the physical body, and the way to move grief out of the body is to *move*. Unfortunately, getting out of bed and going for a walk, practicing yoga, going to the gym, or any physical exercise you typically enjoy becomes difficult amid grief, because we tend to feel exhausted by it. There's no way around it: sweat therapy works, dance movement therapy works. Movement helps us release the blockages and can have enormous benefits on the healing journey.

— **Practice breathwork:** Unprocessed grief creates energetic blockages in the body, and breathwork is another incredible tool to release these blocks and begin to heal.

Breathwork means the practice of conscious deep rhythmic breathing in order to move us into the parasympathetic nervous system and induce a state of calm and relaxation. Breathwork helps us step into our bodies where we innately know how to process grief. It is a beautiful tool to support you on your path to healing.

— **See a medium:** Finding a continued connection with a loved one who has passed on is helpful in healing from grief, and everyone has the ability to make their own direct connections; however, please remember that when we are in the throes of deep sorrow, wanting to make contact more than ever, is when it's hardest to do so. The problem is that grief can lower our vibration, getting in the way of the energy between the person who has passed and us. It is not because grief is *bad*. Grief is necessary. It's because grief energy carries with it a heavy vibration. At the same time, the energetic vibration of spirits is exceptionally strong. Scheduling a session with a medium is an effective way to hear from your loved one and understand firsthand that they are still present and very much a part of your life, especially in the early days when heavy grief causes interference in your communication with the spirit world.

Healing from grief is an attainable goal. There are no time frames or exact ways to grieve. Just know that when you are ready, help is available to you. We all need to go through grief at one point or another. It is important, and we can't rush the process. We can proactively work toward our healing, but to a large degree, it takes as long as it takes. You must remain patient with yourself and your loved ones and be open to them bringing you messages in many unexpected ways. Perhaps a friend of yours who had a recent experience with a medium received a message for you. That doesn't mean your loved one cares more about them than you; it simply means that your friend was available for the message to come through at that time, for whatever reason. Your loved one in the spirit world is waiting for your grief to ease and your vibration to rise enough that they can communicate with you.

On that note, you may also have been told that you must wait for your loved ones to contact you because *they* aren't ready, but that's nonsense. There's no "time" on the other side. We are the ones who need to prepare, not them. And it's okay not to be ready—having grace and patience for yourself is key while you're in the experience of the Dark Night.

We have been created in the most amazing of ways. We are never given more than we can handle, and that includes during life's most challenging moments. Grief comes and goes, and just when we think we cannot take another moment, even when we feel we can't handle another wave of intensive pain, it releases its hold on us long enough to breathe. But the truth is that we *can* endure pain—we are built to. There will be waves of debilitating grief that make you feel like you are drowning, and they will be massive and long-winded waves at first, but they will gradually lessen in intensity over time. But the spirit world also offers us moments of reprieve from the power of grief's grip so we can slowly move forward on the healing path.

Even in deep grief, there are moments gifted to us when we can breathe just a little easier. Does that mean we will never again take a breath like we did before the loss? No. Grief fundamentally changes us, there is no doubt. You never process entirely out of grief. Grief will always be a part of you. But it doesn't have to consume you. It does consume you initially, which is natural, but as time goes on, it moves to that space where it needs to sit in your soul. And when grief sits in your soul, that's when you start to move through it.

Myths about Grief

- The pain will disappear if you ignore it and pretend it isn't there.
- You need to be strong in the face of loss.
- There is a one-year time frame from the beginning to the end of the grieving process.
- Moving on with your life means you have forgotten your loved one.
- You can control your grieving process.
- If people visit, you must be strong and show them you are doing well.
- Crying means you're weak.
- Laughter is wrong when you are in the grieving process.
- Time heals all things.
- Talking about the loss will only make it worse.
- Your pain will bring others down, so you should avoid seeing friends and family.
- If you begin living once again, you will dishonor your loved one.
- Getting over this loss means you didn't love them.
- You will never see them again.

Truths about Grief

- Laughing or joining in life events does not mean you have forgotten them.

- It is okay to talk about your loved ones in spirit, and in fact, it is healthy.

- Grief is not something you can control. Allow the feelings to come when they present themselves.

- Grief will get less intensive with time; however, it doesn't go away.

- You are not crazy.

- The way out of grief is through it.

- Grief is personal.

- It's okay not to be strong.

- You have a right to feel the loss.

- You cannot talk your way out of grief.

- Grief is a normal part of life.

- Grief is like a rollercoaster; it comes and goes.

- People need people; share your grief with trusted friends and family.

- Grief takes longer than most people are aware.

- Grief is not something to solve.

- You do not have to find a "silver lining" when in grief.

- You will see your loved ones again.

I know I'll never quite feel the same after the painful losses I've endured, but I've found ways to fill the holes in my life that loss created. You may fall in love and get married. You may find a new job that fills your time and restores purpose in your life. You may take a leap of faith and move to a new place that you've always wanted to be in and consequently meet the kind of soul friends who feel like family. You will heal because that's what we are designed to do. Not because you're not still grieving, not because you don't still miss them, not because you don't still think of them every single day, but because we are designed to fill the gaps that loss creates with new kinds of love. That is how Spirit is merciful.

In grief, all your senses, emotions, and feelings work overtime to survive the intensive loss. Be gentle with yourself and know that as you go on this healing journey, your loved ones are right beside you, loving you and guiding you through one of your lifetime's most painful—yet spiritually transformative—journeys: loss. Loss is a part of life because love is a part of life. Love and loss are synonymous—if you love, you will lose. You can't have one without the other. That is the reality of being a human.

When we view grief this way, as part of our soul-growth mission here on earth, we can more easily start moving toward healing. Feelings must come up and out; we are fated to feel if we intend to heal. And this has never been truer than with loss. There are no shortcuts to grief— we have to go *through* it. The only cure for grief, it turns out, is to grieve.

IN THEIR OWN WORDS:
Callie F.

It's never easy to lose a loved one, and I lost my dad. The fear of being manipulated by someone made me very skeptical of seeing a medium, but I needed answers. I needed a way to connect with my dad. I was apprehensive, but after reading about Susan, I decided to make an appointment to see her.

I put my husband's name down so that she would have no information to go by if she wasn't honest. She was surprised when I, a female, came in to see her.

Susan was inviting and warm and felt like a friend. Well, let me tell you, my dad came through loud and clear. He not only gave specific names and events but his humor and traits shined through so we could not deny it was really him. She said he was with my grandma and that she met him to assist him in crossing over. She even knew my grandma's nickname. She also was able to name things that only my family could have known.

Susan was able to channel him for us and get answers regarding his passing that no one else could ever know. Susan described black hair and sideburns and big sunglasses and music; she even started doing this silly happy dance my dad used to do. She started to sing an Elvis song, and my mom and I were bawling because that is what my dad sang; he was an Elvis impersonator.

I felt like I was able to speak to my dad for the first time since he died. What a gift and true ability she is sharing with the world. Susan brought us more peace and comfort than I am able to convey. Her gift is truly amazing.

IN THEIR OWN WORDS:
Sal T.

My father was murdered a week before my 15th birthday. Even as I approached 50, the grief was still palpable every day. I always wish my father was able to meet my wife and kids and see my accomplishments. I wanted to believe he knew about these things but never had confirmation. My father immigrated to the U.S. from Mexico when my mother was pregnant with me. As his children were first-generation citizens of the U.S., there were so many dreams my father had for us. I have done more than even I imagined (elected official, business owner, and national educator of the year in 2006), and the angst I felt about not being able to share these accomplishments with him has been a challenge.

My wife found out about Susan on her website and hoped a session would relieve some of the grief I had dealt with since the day my father passed away. The stories from clients were amazing, but I still had a tough time believing mediumship was genuine.

The day we were scheduled for a reading, I felt somewhat nervous because my wife was so excited, and I was thinking, *How am I going to comfort her when we realize this is not legit?* I didn't believe it; however, just before we left for our visit, I was getting dressed and saw a belt of my father's that I had been given recently from my brother. It reminds me of him, and he always wore it—a traditional Mexican-built belt with a large silver belt buckle with a woven strap for the waist. When I saw that belt, I said in my head to my father, "If this is real, you will talk about this belt today." I didn't tell my wife about this.

When we arrived at Susan's office, I was brought into the session space and sat down with Susan. She was kind and explained how the process would flow. As soon as we began the session, Susan stated that she felt a male presence and looked at me with this odd look and said, "There's something about a belt." WHAT?! Shock. And. Awe.

She then said he's been gone for a while. (I even wore black just in case it would make her think he died recently.) She wrote in her journal and asked, "What does the number 15 mean?" I told her I was almost 15 when my father died. She showed me the writing of 15 in her book. That was an amazing way to kick off the experience! I believe that this allowed me to be more relaxed and open about the rest of the information she shared with me.

She then went on to note how he died, the consequence of my father's murderer, and brought forward multiple other family members. One of them was my grandmother, my father's mother, who had more recently passed, and she came through to say she was there, but the family was stepping back so that I could have time with my father.

What a gift. That's the best way I can describe it. The weight removed from my shoulders was remarkable. There is certainly still grief and a sense of loss, but I now believe my father is with me and knows of my success with my family and career.

After this experience, I have shared Susan's contact information and even purchased sessions for friends and family members who have experienced great loss and remain impaled with grief. They, too, have had similar "Shock. And. Awe." experiences. This is a gift that keeps on giving for the rest of my life and many others. Thank you, Susan.

INTEGRATION MOMENT
Grow Through What You Go Through

If you don't deal with life's painful events, they will deal with you. We can start the healing process by acknowledging our grief instead of avoiding it. When you are ready, I invite you to find a safe place where you can be alone, with no distractions, and choose any of the prompts below to begin working through any unresolved or complicated grief you might have.

- Which type of grief are you in? Unexpected? Anticipatory? Complicated?

- In what ways have you helped yourself heal the grief on your journey?

- What are some things you have done to help improve your coping skills in grief?

- What or who have you lost and grieved over? Whether it be death, divorce, infertility, an unwanted move, loss of job, or death of a fur baby, all of these losses and more carry with them a grief cycle.

- After a significant loss, what tools did you use to help you redefine your life goals?

- How well are you functioning in your daily life?

- Do you feel you could have prevented your loved one's death?

- Are you hopeful that you will eventually feel like yourself once again and gain acceptance of your new normal?

Chapter Exercise

Remember, grief is a natural response to loss. All losses can be overwhelming. There is no right or wrong way to grieve. Below are a few suggestions to help you on your path to healing.

- Attend a local grief support group.

- Write out a plan for future holidays, anniversaries, and special days or occasions. These occasions can take you off guard and trigger unmanageable and painful reminders of the loss of your loved one. Having a plan helps!

- Speak out loud to your loved one and have a quiet conversation with them, letting them know how you are feeling and how much you miss them.

- Get enough rest. Rest is vital to healing from the exhaustion of the grief process.

- Move your body. Physical activity can help relieve stress, anxiety, and depression.

- Turn on some music and dance. Movement is healing, energy-releasing behavior that can help relieve stressful moments.

- Visit friends and reach out when possible.

- Write a letter to your loved one who has passed.

CHAPTER 11

Empaths—the Path of the Heart

As an empath, there was never a time in my life when I could avoid picking up on others' emotions. The positive emotions and the negative emotions, it didn't matter. I felt *everything*, and I mean *everything*. Within minutes of walking into a room, I was surrounded by energy and a sense of how the evening would go based on the energy projected by the people in the room. As a child, I frequently felt the energy *before* entering a room. It was as though it penetrated the walls. I often felt the negative first; this was a protective mechanism to gauge my safety.

I didn't yet know how to listen to my instincts but knew what I felt. When something went wrong, I *felt* it, but handling it was a different story. I absorbed it all—the good, the bad, and the ugly—and I would unknowingly pull it into me like a magnet; it was as if an energetic pull created a sense of knowing inside of me. I liken it to carrying a heavy weight on a pulley that could pull me up and down depending on the mood I was sensing around me.

It's more than likely you are an empath if you have also felt this way since you can remember. However, that would make you a unique minority. While most people (sans sociopaths) have the ability, in varying degrees, to *feel* empathetic toward others, according to a 2007 study on empathy published in *Nature Neuroscience*, only 1 to 2 percent of the population are *true* empaths.* If that number sounds low to you, that's because it has become quite trendy nowadays for people to be quick to label themselves as empaths. But there is a big difference between having the *ability* to be empathetic toward others and being what I call an "empath soul"—people whose core *identity* is built on a compassionate foundation.

Having an Empath Soul vs. Empathetic Qualities

Empath souls embody the qualities and traits of empathy on a deep and fundamental level; empathy is the main attribute of their being. The term *empath* derives from the Greek words *em* (in) and *pathos* (feeling). While someone with empathetic *qualities* might very well possess a heightened ability to sense and feel the emotions, energy, and experiences of others, empath *souls* constantly live "in feeling."

Empath souls step into the feelings of others; they are not just able to put themselves in another's shoes, they automatically do so by *default*, often to the point of having difficulty focusing on self-needs rather than others' needs.

While most people live life from their internal emotional world and project it outward, empath souls live,

---

*Michael J. Banissy and Jamie Ward, "Mirror-Touch Synesthesia Is Linked with Empathy," *Nature Neuroscience, 10* (August 2007): 815–6. https://www.researchgate.net/publication/6263804_Mirror-touch _synesthesia_is_linked_with_empathy.

conversely, from the *outside in*, openly feeling what is outside of them, which in turn affects the feelings inside of them. They are absorbers of the tensions, heartaches, and happiness of the energy around them.

People who are not empath souls—again, this is most people—filter their life experiences primarily through the mind. They think, analyze, employ logic, and then they *feel*. Conversely, empaths filter their experiences primarily through the heart. They sense, feel, engage emotion, and then they *think*.

For instance, if I were to talk about an emotional event in my life, like the loss of my grandmother, most people would understand and relate to my sadness. That could be because I have shared my experience with them, or they may have endured a similar loss themselves. They will most likely feel empathetic feelings toward me because I've told them a sad story of loss. They might even cry with me, but they will filter my account through their knowing, thinking brains. "I know Susan is sad and grieving, and I understand why, and my heart goes out to her."

An empath will not only know what I am experiencing but also will be able to feel it internally. They won't just *know* I'm grieving and feel sad for me; they will *feel* my grief. They will cry with me not because I told them I'm hurting but because the pain becomes so relatable that the empath feels compassionate toward the experience.

I wanted to start this chapter with the above distinction because it's an extremely important one. Not everyone is a natural empath, and not everyone is meant to be. It is important to note that empathy is a spectrum, and research has found that empathy is a trait people can develop throughout their lives.

The Characteristics of an Empath

I will use the term "empath" for the remainder of the chapter to denote both the rare empath souls and the many others living with heightened empathic qualities—all individuals with a high sensitivity to the emotions, energy, and experiences of those around them. If you identify as such, this chapter will help you learn the proper tools to manage your emotional bodies and soft sides in an increasingly hardened world.

As I shared earlier, I do not remember a time when I didn't feel *everything*. I spent so much of my life trying to heal everything and everyone that I disregarded the importance of healing myself. I wanted the world to be a safe place. I wanted it to be kind, loving, and thoughtful. Most of the time, it was, but other times, it was harsh and confusing.

Before discussing how to manage this beautiful, puzzling gift, let me give you some clear-cut answers to what an empath feels. Everywhere we go, people tend to pour their hearts out to us. Even strangers are attracted to the gentle energy that we give off. It happens without any forewarning. Because an empath has a natural magnetic pull, people tend to move toward us for comfort, solace, understanding, and a kind ear. They share intimate details with us even when they have just met us. They trust us, and they should; we are kind souls who genuinely care about the pain of others. We respond with love, respect, and understanding toward their feelings. Empaths must use caution as we tend to feel others' feelings before we realize we have picked up their energy. The following are some common traits of empaths.

— **We are sensitives:** Being *a* sensitive is very different from the trait of being overly sensitive. We are sensitives; we feel and respond to the sensitivities in the world. Empaths can be overwhelmed with feelings, both our own and others. We know what others are trying to communicate without ever saying a word. So it stands to reason that we would feel all the emotions around us and quickly become overwhelmed. We share our love and time with others, and our energy is desperately needed in this realm we inhabit.

— **We want the truth:** Empaths know and feel the energy of a lie. When someone is not speaking the truth to us, we want to doubt our truth, which tends to confuse us, but we *do* know it. We suffer over people lying to us and tend to take it on as if we caused it.

— **We hold on to horror stories:** Once we feel it, we cannot *un-feel* it. We get overwhelmed when we are told the horrors of the world. We avoid negative images like the plague. If someone shares a painful story, we will react internally, and it will imprint on our minds for months, sometimes for years to come. Even a commercial can affect us if it depicts any suffering.

— **We believe peace occurs through healing:** Empaths are helpers and healers. Even as children, we wanted everything to be happy and healthy. We walk you through all the feelings you are feeling to some degree. If you're not feeling well physically, feeling overwhelming sadness, depression, or agitation, we are going through all those emotions with you and want to help. We're connected to those we care about, and we care about almost everyone.

— **We are anxious:** We have a strong tendency toward anxiety in large crowds, even if we feel comfortable in them. We *feel* the room's energy, and it heightens our energy, which sometimes creates stress. When we leave, we wear others' feelings, so we must be cautious not to put on others' coats of emotions.

— **We are the go-to people:** We will listen and share for hours on end, and when things get the best of us, we listen and share some more. We have a naturally wise answer to your concerns and confusion. This is a gift we have called the gift of discernment, and we *want* to share it with others.

— **We are loyal to a fault:** If you hurt us, we will forgive you repeatedly. We are great forgetters, so when you repeat behaviors that harm us or others and say you are sorry, we *believe* you. We want everyone to be their best, so we see them as their best self. When they prove us wrong, it is heartbreaking and shocking to us. If you tell us you have changed, we believe you because you said it.

— **We are intuitive:** We feel who you are before we meet you. We know whether you are safe or not. We don't always listen because we tend to see the best in others even when shown differently, but we still feel who you are. Don't be fooled by our softness; we are wiser than you think. Our intuition tells us the next right thing to do; however, we don't always listen to that little voice inside us because our tenderness gets in the way.

— **We love animals, and they love us:** We tend to lean in to them for solace, and they offer it gladly. We have a natural bond with them; we communicate with them without needing to speak. They are our family, not our pets. As a child, when an animal was sick or needed me, I would hold it for hours upon hours to help it "feel better."

— **We are very often bullied and not part of the crowd:** We are usually looking from the outside in. I liken it to looking through a window, watching others, and wanting to be like them so we can fit in and be a part of the fun.

Empath Children

Thinking back to the heart's "little brain" discussed in Chapter 8, you can think of an empath as someone who is led primarily by the heart-brain, the "seat of the soul." They first sense the world around them with their souls. I call them "soul seers" because they see *with* their souls and see the soul in *everything*. Once developed and understood, being an empath and recognizing your heart-brain connection is a gift. But in an overtly logical world, you can imagine how this can feel like a cross to bear, particularly to children and young adults. Natural-born empathic children will undoubtedly have a more difficult time in the early stages of their life.

As a child, I remember this deep longing to belong and fit in. I was tender and sensitive. I wanted everyone to love me, and I did everything possible to make that happen. I was so young and small, yet I knew that people needed to talk and cry. I knew when they were in pain physically and emotionally, and I wanted to make them well. I carried a lot of fear because emotionally sensing everything around you can be very intense. I often felt anxious and afraid of physical and emotional hurt, yet I was a healer. I loved everything and everyone, and I was sure they loved me!

It took many years and countless tears to recognize the power and beauty within my empath soul. I tried to heal every broken thing. But as I went through life and realized how different I was from others, I started to see myself as the most broken of all.

Seeing our children overwhelmed is such a painful and powerless feeling. Especially if we feel we can do nothing to make it better for them. But remember that their empathic energy is what makes them the unique and loving souls they are. Offering your empath child patience and love will help them learn to not only understand their gift but also to see what is right in their world.

Growing up, I was fortunate to have other empaths in my home, and I thank God for that now. I don't know how life might have looked for me had I not felt support in this way. I believe that made me feel like a part of the whole. Offering your child guidance at home can make a huge difference in their journey. Counseling, mentors, and other resources can significantly benefit them.

Empath children may need help productively sharing their feelings and that means providing safe and supportive spaces. With support, the empathic child can grow and expand their gifts and ultimately become healers in the world. There are different rules of engagement for an empathic child. Learning how to manage the intensity of their feelings is of the utmost importance.

As a child, I wanted the world to be safe, kind, loving, and thoughtful, but I often found it harsh and confusing. I found myself attracted to people who were *not* kind and caring—learning to distinguish who is kind and loving and who is cruel and selfish is the *right of passage* for the empath to grow and come fully into the magnificence of their superpower.

Supporting Your Empath Child

Empathy is the medicine the world needs, and your empath child is a beautiful and unique soul here to deliver that medicine. However, the floods of stimuli coming into their souls can leave children and young adults feeling depressed, especially if they don't receive support along the journey to understanding and growing into their empathic nature. With your love and guidance, I assure you they can learn to navigate the world with confidence and grace. Guide them to utilize their empathy to help the world as they were destined to. Here are some ways you can support your empath child:

- Make sure their home environment is safe.
- Teach them how to handle situations that are baffling them.
- As with all empaths, teaching them self-care is essential.
- Show them how to set boundaries—and make sure you teach them through example.
- Teach them how to say "NO"; this is necessary for self-care and self-esteem.
- Show them how to remove themselves from situations or environments where they feel uncomfortable.
- Most important, show them love and acceptance. With your help, they will learn to navigate their empathic energy, and as they learn to understand it in its totality, they will ultimately thrive in it!

If you feel overwhelmed by your child's empathic abilities, consider seeking resources for your child, such as therapy or support groups. That can help them connect with others who share their experience and learn additional coping mechanisms.

Beware of Narcissists

Narcissists often enter the world of the empath, and an unhealthy dance occurs between them. Narcissists are attracted to empaths because they see them as having the ability to care for their needs and fill their large hole, so to speak. They look to be validated, and empaths are extremely good at validating others.

Like empathy, narcissism exists on a spectrum. Those with narcissistic traits are not necessarily diagnosed as narcissists, which can be confusing. A true narcissist has an extreme sense of entitlement; they are manipulative and self-centered. Remember that narcissists can also be intuitive, creating a situation where they gain the empath's trust. Imagine how vulnerable empaths are to the allure of the narcissist and the emotional harm the narcissist can cause. Empaths consistently meet the needs of others; their souls are so extremely open and forgiving.

We tend to think of empaths as altruistic, but sometimes they can have ulterior motives. In truth, there is a payoff to being reasonable and accommodating; it helps us to feel worthy and lovable. When you think about it, there's nothing better than being loved and seen as extraordinary. However, the empath usually does good deeds for others because they sincerely care about the human condition. I have come to realize that it is prudent to suggest empathic people ask their higher self, "Who is this person I am with?" If they pause long enough, they will see the truth and know if they're dealing with a narcissistic personality.

A true narcissist can appear overly charming, so it can be difficult to recognize them. It's necessary to ensure what we're dealing with when we're out in the world. What I see most often is that the empath will remain in a situation where they continuously give of themselves without any reciprocity. That can be very damaging to the empath's soul over the years. Keep in mind, whether or not the empath is emotionally harmed, they will heal as healing comes naturally and is their superpower. They can forgive the person who caused them harm and do so with love, but they never forget. It can be particularly challenging for them; however, their constitution to remain humbled and healed is stronger than even they are aware.

Narcissists love to use the phrase, "You're *too* sensitive!" Empaths hear this phrase so much throughout their lives that a whole chapter could be written on this phrase alone! For an empath, it is doubtful they are being "too sensitive." I've reached the point where I've heard this so many times that I now respond, "You are correct—*I am a sensitive!*" Remember, their sensitivity is their strength. Narcissists throw it around as if it's an insult, but the truth is that our sensitivity isn't what's wrong with us—it innately opens the door to our knowing, our intuition, if we will listen.

The acknowledgment of our intuition, then, allows us to recognize that sensitivity isn't what is *wrong* with us, but it *is* what is *right* with us! Empaths understand the world around them on a deep level, lead with their hearts, and see with their souls—this is something to be *proud* of, not ashamed of. Reframing this and seeing your empathic nature as a strength rather than a weakness is extremely important on the empath's journey. The great news is that if you know how to understand and navigate your sensitive nature, being an empath will become the richest gift of your life.

Here are a few tools the empath can use to minimize the damage of the narcissistic relationship, protect their well-being, and avoid allowing narcissists to enter their world:

— **Set boundaries:** Learn to say no! Setting clear boundaries isn't about the other person not crossing you, because they may; it's about knowing what you will do when they cross you and then following through with that plan. When dealing with a narcissist, limit your time with them. Keep your distance the best you can once you recognize what you're dealing with.

— **Practice self-care:** Empaths must learn to transmute their worldly challenge into their spiritual superpower. How do they do this? Self-care. It sounds simple, but it isn't easy. Empaths need to learn to take care of their emotional well-being *first*. It is our duty to learn how to protect our emotional bodies. It is a requirement on our soul's path in this lifetime. Self-care is the number one key to recognizing your choices. If you are overtired or overbusy, you won't take the time to notice the people around you. Meditation, breathwork, good rest, and exercise can help you with your focus, enabling you to take note of what's happening in your relationships with others.

— **Connect with other empaths:** Work on your self-esteem. One of the ways to do that is to be around other empaths who will encourage you and build you up. You can do the same for them. So search out like-minded people.

— **Practice empathy without absorbing others' emotions:** Learning to avoid internalizing others' feelings is difficult for the empath. Learning to have compassion and concern for others but not internalize their feelings is essential. That will not be easy, but it can be done with practice.

— **Seek professional support:** If you feel that you are having difficulty separating your emotions from a narcissistic relationship and creating an environment of safety, it might be time for you to seek outside intervention. A great support system can be the catalyst for expanded awareness and growth.

By learning to set boundaries, prioritize self-care, practice empathy without absorbing others' emotions, and seek professional support when needed, empaths can function effectively in the world while staying true to their unique abilities and sensitivities.

Are All Mediums Empaths?

Remember, empaths are healers; our world *needs* to focus on humanity's love and healing, and to do so, we must have humane people. Empaths are just that— mindful healers who have the ability to make this world a better place. They are found in every profession—doctors, artists, teachers, and so on. And many, of course, take the spiritual path as I did.

People often ask me, "Are all mediums empaths?" It might surprise some people to know that the answer is a perplexing *no*! I wish I could answer this important question by saying the opposite is true, and I've often struggled to come to terms with this myself. I want to believe that all mediums are empaths, considering the sensitive nature of the job. Unfortunately, I've met my fair share of mediums who were not empathetic and even possessed narcissistic tendencies. That is why you must use caution when inviting a medium into your spiritual energy field.

How to Discern If a Medium Is Legitimate

There are so many legitimate mediums out there, both the empath-soul kinds and the empathetic kinds, who only want to help people heal, but there are also plenty of fraudulent ones with not-so-good intentions. As with any industry, a few bad seeds can give the majority a bad name.

Signs of a Questionable Medium

- They may say there are curses or attachments that need to be removed from your body.
- They give you only general information.
- They ask for more money to help them remove a negative entity.
- They have a lack of transparency.
- They try to instill fear in you.
- If it sounds too good to be true, it probably is.

Remember: The spirit world is love, and they give messages accordingly! Do your homework; if it feels off, it probably is.

Signs of a Legitimate Spiritual Medium

- They have a history of positive testimonials and reviews.
- They put your well-being first and foremost.
- They are educated regarding ethics.
- They provide specific, mostly accurate, and meaningful information.
- They will not ask for more money.
- They won't encourage you to return every week or month.
- They are educated in their field and understand grief.
- They will not come from a place of fear and warnings.

Remember: Mediums are having a human experience also. No medium has 100 percent accuracy, even the best ones. If you are receiving inaccurate information, let them know. At that point, a medium with integrity and ethics will stop the reading and offer a refund.

There is so much to say about empaths; I could fill the pages of a complete book. For now, I want to end by stating this important point: empaths are gifts to humanity and should be protected at all costs. Whether you're the parent of an empath, a friend of an empath, or an empath yourself, please understand that empaths aren't broken; it's the collective heart of society that is broken. Empaths are tasked to help us mend it.

They are here to help us see in a new way. While most people are mind-driven, an empath's world revolves around the heart, and it's the heart that heals and helps. I would like to repeat this one more time: child empaths or adult empaths who don't yet understand their gift believe that something is wrong with them, when in truth, something is extremely right with them.

Our world tends to rely on facts, science, and logic. Our empathic energy depends on our souls knowing. Truth lies somewhere between fact and feeling. Therefore, empathic energy is an excellent asset to us. Regardless of the narrative that strong sensitivity is our weakness, it is the empath's greatest gift to the world.

Feeling the world around you intensely, seeing with your soul, and leading with love is not a weakness. We can all agree that this world could use a lot more heart. That's what empaths are here for—to pioneer a better way of being for humankind. Whether you consider yourself an empath or not, reaching toward more empathy in your life, the heart-led path, and more love, will be pivotal in your soul's growth during this lifetime.

IN THEIR OWN WORDS:
Victoria

When I first met Susan, my daughter, Mia, was going through an incredibly challenging time in her young life. She had been the target of relentless bullying, and it seemed like she was carrying the weight of the world on her shoulders. She also was seeing things in her room at night and having trouble sleeping. She wasn't relating to the other children and would come home crying that she hated her life. We were afraid and heartbroken for her. Little did we know that there was something extraordinary about Mia—she had the gift of the empath and the ability to see spirits.

From the moment we stepped into Susan's office, I could sense her genuine care and understanding for Mia. Susan projects an instant energy of love, and she has an obvious sixth sense about her—an innate ability to comprehend the depths of Mia's pain and struggles. She listened with loving concern and created a safe space where Mia felt comfortable opening up about her pain, fears, and confusion.

Susan's unique blend of compassion, wisdom, and expertise from her own life experiences allowed her to identify with Mia and her gifts. She immediately began to equip her with the tools she needed to navigate her emotions and embrace her abilities. Watching Mia transform under Susan's guidance was awe-inspiring. With each session, she grew stronger, more confident, and more at peace with herself. I grew to learn about Mia's gifts, and Susan taught me how to help my daughter flourish.

The profound impact of Susan's support became evident in the way Mia began to smile, laugh, and gain confidence. No longer burdened by fear, she embraced her gift of empathy, and her connection to spirits became a source of excitement rather than dread. Susan empowered Mia to see her unique qualities as strengths and encouraged her to explore her true calling as a healer.

Over the course of our monthly visits, Susan became an integral part of Mia's journey to healing and self-discovery. Even after a year of regular sessions, Mia would ask to see Susan whenever she felt overwhelmed or needed guidance. Susan's dedication to Mia's well-being and her genuine interest in her growth has been nothing short of life-changing.

Today, Mia is an 18-year-old woman who radiates confidence, compassion, and a deep sense of purpose. She has found her passion in healing and is dedicated to helping others with her gifts—a transformation I attribute directly to Susan's invaluable guidance.

In a sea of counselors (of which we saw many before seeing Susan), Susan stands out as a true healer. Her ability to understand and connect with Mia on such a profound level is a gift in itself. As a parent, I will forever be grateful for the positive impact Susan has had on my daughter's life and our entire family.

I wholeheartedly recommend Susan Grau to anyone seeking a compassionate, skilled, and insightful guide on their journey to healing and self-discovery. Her commitment to her client's well-being and genuine desire to make a difference in their lives is remarkable.

Thank you, Susan, for being the guiding light that helped my daughter find her way through the darkness and embrace her unique gifts. Your support has been a blessing beyond words, and we are forever grateful for your presence in our lives.

INTEGRATION MOMENT
Getting in Tune with Your Empathy

Even if you do not consider yourself an empath after reading this chapter, you can always become more empathic. The following questions can help you reflect on this:

- What have you learned about yourself and your energy from reading this chapter?
- Do you have trouble telling people no? Does the word make you uncomfortable?
- How can you better navigate your surroundings to feel a part of things?
- Do you feel that you have been on the outside looking in most of your life?
- Have you been told you are "too sensitive" and need to "toughen up"?
- Do you absorb others' energy?
- Are you highly attached to nature and animals?
- Do you take care of others at your own expense?
- Are you the go-to person when others are in need?

Chapter Exercises

Being an empath has been the greatest gift of my life and the most difficult to navigate. It took me years to feel like I belonged in this world. Once I understood how to manage my emotions and attachments to people, places, and things, I began recognizing my own personal empowerment. Let's look at ways that you can expand your awareness of your empathic energy:

- Start learning about empathic energy. Make a commitment to yourself to learn about empathic traits to better understand how you are different and the same as others.

- Write down all the traits you have learned about and begin the process of self-awareness.

- Find a quiet space and journal to better understand who you are as an empath and how that has affected your life journey.

- Do you have family members that you see as empathic? If so, begin a conversation about different ways and strategies you have used to better cope with the world around you.

- Practice mindful meditation for 15 mins a day, even if that is when you crawl into bed at the end of the day.

- Take "time out" when you feel overwhelmed in any environment to readjust and reset.

- We empaths tend to hold our breath often, so breathe. If you have anxiety, ask yourself what is happening around you and if you are absorbing someone else's energy. If the answer is yes, try to learn and practice mindful breathwork.

- Write down positive affirmations about yourself and repeat them daily.

- For 30 days, commit to writing down one thing you love about yourself.

Remember: Being an empath is the most beautiful energy that a soul can carry. Yes, it has challenges, but that is part of self-actualization and growth. This chapter was written for all the empaths who never felt a part of the group! It is your time; be the gift you were created to be!

CHAPTER 12

The Gift of Life

One in 400 trillion—those are the odds of you being born. A probability so low that it's effectively zero. The odds of winning the lottery is 1 in 300 million, which means the likelihood of your birth equates to winning the lottery 1.33 million times! If you were a betting person, you would never bet on your life with those odds. It would take a miracle to win, to be born—and yet, here you are. It *is* a miracle. *You* are a miracle.

While this human life may often seem like a headache and heartache, the more profound spiritual truth is that you *chose* to be here. To be alive in your human form, to be challenged, to experience duality are all things your soul *desires*. The ups, the downs. The lessons, the blessings. The dark, the light. You wanted it all—and it's *all* a gift.

Through this gift of life, we are granted a significant opportunity that we don't have in the world of spirit: to experience the *entire* spectrum of emotions. Not only the blissful ones that make up the beautiful spirit world but also the darker ones that don't exist there: sorrow, pain, jealousy, anger, and even hate. And while a life without the darker emotions might sound incredible to us here on earth, where things often feel too heavy, our souls *need* to experience those emotions to become fully actualized. Darkness, after all, makes the light shine brighter. Here, in our human lifetime, we have the privilege to feel it all, learn through contrast, and grow. We have the chance to experience love directly—after all, how can we truly know love if we have never met hate?

When we embrace this point of view—that human life is a precious opportunity for our soul's evolution, perceived challenges and all—we can experience the world in a new and profound way. Not only are we then able to appreciate the beauty and wonder of the natural world, savor the simple moments of life, and connect with others in deep and meaningful ways, but we can also begin to intentionally walk our soul's path and align more effectively with our unique life's purpose that's been laid out for us by Spirit—to walk our personalized Yellow Brick Road.

Your Soul's Path

I have found the majority of spiritual literature focuses on the concept that "we are all one." And that's undoubtedly true. But it's equally important to understand that although we are all part of the same spiritual ocean, so to speak, we are still unique, individualized drops of water in that ocean. No one is like you. Not one other soul! Even identical twins are not entirely identical; their DNA reveals two distinct patterns.

We are all made of the same matter—bones, hairs, organs—yet we are each individualized expressions of a unified whole. Every part of you has been created solely for you by Spirit. And it's when we recognize that every aspect of us is unique and has something to offer, something no one else on the entire planet has, we begin the important pilgrimage of self-discovery—a journey that ultimately leads us to find our assigned purpose in this lifetime.

One of the most common questions my clients ask me, and one you are probably wondering, is: "What is my soul purpose?" My answer to them and you is that our collective soul path is a journey of self-exploration, and at its core lies the practice of self-love. We are here, every single one of us, to become masters at loving ourselves. Learning to love ourselves is the great mission of our lives, and it is the path we must follow to effectively understand and excel at fulfilling our life's purpose of serving humanity. In other words: Every person on the planet's *soul purpose* is to master self-love, and walking that path will, in time, reveal your specific *life purpose*—the one that is meant for you and only you.

That self-love is vital to our spiritual development probably isn't shocking news. At the core of our collective consciousness, we *know* that self-love is the key to many of life's significant locks—which can be seen in timelessly viral axioms such as "you can't truly love another until you fully love yourself." While that sentiment makes sense upon initial glance, I don't believe it is entirely accurate. We actually come here with a strong ability to love other people; it is in loving ourselves that things get messy.

Lack of self-love doesn't prevent us from loving other people—I've known many people who possess minuscule amounts of self-love that can shower tons of love onto others wonderfully. What lack of self-love *actually* does is prevent *us* from receiving love from other people, because if you don't love yourself, you won't believe that you deserve love from others.

Whichever way you look at it, the fact remains that learning self-love is crucial on the path to spiritual mastery.

We each have an individualized Yellow Brick Road to follow, but self-love is the foundation of every single one of those paths. So, what does self-love mean, exactly, and how can we cultivate more of it in our lives?

The Meaning of Self-Love

When you hear the term *self-love*, images of getting a massage and taking a hot bath bomb soak in the tub might come to mind. And while these self-care rituals can undoubtedly be beneficial (and wonderful!), the path to cultivating true self-love requires much more than that. That's because self-love isn't just about feeling good—it's about, more than anything, feeling *worthy*.

As humans, feeling unworthy is a universal problem. In childhood, we each had a core wound that took root and caused us to feel unworthy of something, possibly everything, as adults—whether it be love, success, happiness, and so on. This feeling of unworthiness often grows into self-loathing as it accumulates throughout our lives. The practice of loving ourselves, then, becomes a panacea for every core wound of unworthiness that exists— because the result of increased self-love is recognizing on a soul level that we are inherently worthy of love and acceptance. It is our birthright to be loved and accepted, and self-love is the path that teaches us this truth. *Self-love is the only effective weapon to combat self-hate.*

To love ourselves—it sounds so simple, yet if it were, we wouldn't have a massively thriving self-help and therapy industry, and I wouldn't be writing this chapter! The truth is that for people who have experienced childhood trauma or other negative experiences in the course of their lives (read: all of us!), developing true self-love is easier said than done. Many therapists report that lack of self-love is the number one issue they see among their clients— the root of all their surface issues—and it's when we learn to tend to that root and better love ourselves that all the other problem areas in our lives begin to correct themselves as a result.

Our souls are here to learn self-love, but until we do, our lives are chock-full of self-loathing. We are all hardest on ourselves. Each our own worst critics, we give ourselves a harder time than anyone else ever could. Prior to waking up to the power of our thoughts, the conversations inside of our heads tend to be significantly derogatory. If someone in your life treated you the way you treat yourself, you would have taken them out with the trash long ago! But by beginning to think intentionally loving, kind, and compassionate thoughts about ourselves, we take the first step on the journey to self-love. As the iconic Louise Hay said, "You have been criticizing yourself for years, and it hasn't worked. Try approving of yourself and see what happens."

I won't lead you to believe that learning to love yourself is easy—it has personally been the work of my life, and it likely will be for you too. It requires us to confront our deepest fears and vulnerabilities and to let go of the beliefs, patterns, and behaviors that no longer serve our highest good. It is difficult work, but it is worth every ounce of effort. To make it slightly easier, remember to give yourself grace as you embark on the self-love journey— mastery never happens overnight. As with everything, practice makes perfect, and I encourage you to commit to a self-love routine as if you were training for a marathon. When we begin to practice self-love regularly, our self-love muscle strengthens, and the effects are nothing short of life-changing. And, as with any muscle, you have to work it for the rest of your life to stay strong; it's not a one-and-done situation. You've got to train to gain.

A commitment to self-love asks a lot of us, absolutely, but the rewards are profound when we are willing to do the work. Upleveling in the self-love department means we become more connected to our true selves and naturally start to navigate the ups and downs of life with more grace and ease; we become more resilient when the going gets tough in the face of adversity; and, most important, we begin to connect with our highest selves and align with our grand purpose in this lifetime. Learning to love ourselves and finding our life's purpose go hand in hand—and our Yellow Brick Road truly starts to light up for us as we grow and nurture our love of *self*.

Self-Love Practices

Beyond tending to our thoughts, self-love also means engaging in practices that support our physical, emotional, and spiritual well-being. Developing more self-love in our lives means choosing to spend our time supporting ourselves on every level. Here are some ideas to get you started on the path to self-love:

Physically

- Practice yoga.
- Join a gym.
- Take morning or evening walks.
- Get plenty of sleep.
- Eat healthy foods.

Mentally

- Practice positive affirmations.
- Read personal development books.
- Commit to regular therapy sessions.
- Study mindset mastery.
- Learn something new.

Emotionally

- Begin a morning journaling routine.
- Prioritize activities that make you laugh.
- Practice random acts of kindness.
- Sign up to volunteer.
- Practice learning to say "no" and boundary setting.

Spiritually

- Begin a regular meditation practice.
- Start your day with a gratitude list.
- Enroll in a creative class.
- Spend more time in nature.
- Practice visualization techniques.

This is just a small sample of possibilities; the options are truly endless. The point is that it's your job *to choose* to stop feeding yourself things that hurt your soul and begin investing in things that empower you—things that *light* you up! Whichever practices you adopt, repeatedly choosing them will rewire your negative thoughts, patterns, and behaviors toward yourself, resulting in you naturally starting to fall in love with the *you* in you!

The Role of Forgiveness in Self-Love

One of the most important—though definitely not the easiest—components of developing more self-love is learning to forgive ourselves and others for past mistakes and hurts. Forgiveness holds the remarkable power to facilitate healing.

When we hold onto feelings like anger or resentment toward another person—or ourselves—we are holding on to negative energy, which ultimately weighs us down and prevents us from living life to the fullest and forming deep and meaningful relationships. When we choose forgiveness, we release all the negative energy, which in turn creates more room for love, acceptance, and compassion.

Self-forgiveness involves letting go of the weight of past mistakes, acknowledging our humanity, and extending compassion and empathy to ourselves. It is a transformative act that enables personal growth. On the other hand, forgiveness of others allows us to release the grip of anger and resentment, offering a path toward understanding, reconciliation, and rebuilding trust. By embracing these acts of forgiveness, we create a fertile ground for emotional and spiritual healing, allowing wounds to mend, hearts to mend, and a sense of wholeness to emerge.

A big myth says forgiveness means condoning someone's destructive behaviors. But forgiveness, in truth, doesn't mean you co-sign negative behavioral patterns; instead, it means you are ready to heal and be free of the things that limit you and hold you back from stepping into your peace and power. Forgiveness is not only for the person who harmed you but also for you. When we choose to forgive someone for the pain they have directly or indirectly caused us, it is a powerful act of self-love. It means we are choosing to prioritize our own mental and emotional health. True forgiveness sets us free—and that is a gift in and of itself.

But Isn't Self-Love Selfish?

It's important to talk about the self-love-is-selfish conundrum. Self-love often gets an unwarranted reputation because it's wrongly confused with selfishness, but I assure you there is nothing selfish about self-love. In fact, it is the only way we can effectively tend to our spiritual gifts and serve our fellow humans the way in which Spirit intends for us. As author Parker Palmer explains in her book *Let Your Life Speak*, "Self-care is never a selfish act—it is simply good stewardship of the only gift I have, the gift I was put on earth to offer others." When we take the time to listen to our inner selves and prioritize our needs, we can better impact the lives of those around us.

Self-love isn't about seeing yourself and your needs as more important than others. It's about seeing yourself *as good as and as important as* as other people. We've all heard the saying "treat others as you wish to be treated"—it's the Golden Rule, after all, popular among all religious doctrines. Ultimately, self-love asks us to apply the Golden Rule to ourselves as well: Treat yourself as valuable and worthwhile and deserving as you treat the people you love most.

Self-love, at the core, is the process of remembering that we are all inherently worthy of love and acceptance from ourselves and others, and thus self-love is the act of loving and accepting ourselves just as we are. True self-love is complete self-acceptance, and when we accept ourselves fully, flaws and all, we are able to see that we are indeed worthy of all good things. That doesn't mean we don't strive to grow and be better people every single day—of course we do! Self-acceptance simply means that we learn to treat ourselves with compassion, grace, and respect, and care for ourselves on every level—physically, emotionally, mentally, spiritually.

Self-love isn't selfish; it's the core ingredient for creating a fulfilling, meaningful life and aligning with our life's primary purpose. Learning to love ourselves is the most important thing we are here to do—and it is the most difficult. It's a process of continually choosing against our default way of thinking, which is to be hard on ourselves, and to instead choose grace.

All of life is making choices, and when we engage in practices that support our physical, emotional, and spiritual health, authentic self-love begins to flow in for us. We treat ourselves the way we want others to treat us, and by doing that, we attract more of that energy into our lives. When we take time to listen to our inner voice and prioritize our spiritual needs, we benefit, which allows us to positively benefit the lives of those around us—there's nothing selfish about it!

Finding Your Life Purpose

If you were an anthropologist studying the Western world, you would conclude that we collectively think the purpose of our lives is to overwork ourselves with work we dread, all to amass loads of money and never even get to really enjoy it because we are too busy, too tired, and too stressed. It's not a pretty picture, yet it's one we know all too well. More and more, though, people are waking up to the fact that there is more to life than that spiritually fruitless hamster wheel. Our souls aren't here to burn out with meaningless work for decades of our life, only to retire too exhausted to truly live the life we always felt called to in our souls. The secret to being released from that toxic-to-our-soul system and heeding the call of our souls is to discover and embody our spiritual life's purpose.

Each and every one of us has a mission to fulfill in this life—a purpose that we are meant to discover, embody, and master. Once again, self-love is *the* path to the revelation of that purpose. Every step you take toward loving yourself unconditionally, no matter how small, is a step toward discovering that ultimate purpose—your one-of-a-kind gift that only you can offer the world. If you think you are someone who has no gifts, I promise you that you are wrong! We *all* come into this life with spiritual gifts and are *all* meant to share those gifts with the world. When we stifle those gifts, our souls suffer, and our spiritual missions in this lifetime are left unfulfilled.

Remember that our souls are crafted with great precision by Spirit, which means we come equipped with various talents and abilities that help us uncover and fulfill our life purpose. Though each of our life purposes varies and is custom-made for us, they all share in common the concept that each of us is here as part of something bigger than ourselves and that our lives have meaning beyond the day-to-day struggles and challenges we face. We are part of a great mysterious spiritual puzzle; doing our piece is crucial. There is more to life, and as we cultivate more self-love and acceptance, develop our spirit consciousness, and nurture our relationship with the spirit world, we open ourselves up to that "more" and show Spirit that we are ready for the revealing of our spiritual gifts and thus to answer the call of our life's purpose.

It might sound contradictory that our soul's purpose is self-love and our life's purpose is to serve others, but the goal is to unite them—to integrate truly loving yourself with lovingly serving humanity in your own unique way. All of life is a balance between self and others, and once we do the work to strike that balance in our lives, we will see life for the *true* gift that it is.

I didn't always see this messy human life as a gift. The journey from my childhood experiences to my life as a professional medium was long, confusing, and often painful. For many years, I didn't want to be on this planet, with all the pain and inequalities that exist. But today, after walking my own path toward self-love and self-acceptance, exactly as I am, cracks and all, I have found my life's purpose. Now I *know* with every bone in my body that my life is a gift. I am here for a reason, and I am so grateful that I am.

My life journey has been a profound awakening that my soul is meant to love and grow amidst even the worst of adversity. I now have a deep appreciation for the gifts I have been given—the ones I have come to see bright and clear *because of* the dark times—and a deep understanding of the role they play in fulfilling my unique purpose of serving humanity. Yes, I have struggled along the way, as we all do. But I am genuinely grateful for that struggle, for it is what motivated me, ultimately, to bloom. I hope that by sharing my story, I can inspire you to walk your soul path, embrace the gifts you find along the way, and live a life filled with love, compassion, and purpose.

❀ ❀ ❀

When you embrace both the pains and joys of this journey, you will start to understand that every single moment of this life is a gift meant to be celebrated, and it is the journey itself that is the ultimate gift—living, dying, and the in-between. Each moment is a chance to grow, to learn, and to deepen our connection to both the human world and the world of spirit. When we treat life as the gift it is, when the time comes to transition back to the other side of the veil, we will be proud that we have fulfilled our soul purpose and brought love and healing to those around us. While it's true that life can be rife with challenges, being alive right here, right now, is a true blessing. We are fortunate to be here, experiencing all the ups and downs that come with the human experience. With a positive mindset and a grateful heart, we can embrace the challenges we have and appreciate the gift of life we have chosen.

Remember: 1 in 400 trillion. Your life is a gift. You are a miracle. Live accordingly.

INTEGRATION MOMENT
Love Yourself First

If you are currently on a journey of self-discovery, growth, and finding your life's purpose, it is essential to understand that the heart of this journey lies within you. Self-love is such an important endeavor that writer June Jordan went so far as to say, "I must undertake to love myself and respect myself as though my very life depends upon self-love and self-respect."* According to Spirit, Jordan's musing is spot-on—we are meant to commit to walking the path of self-love first and foremost in our lifetimes.

Choose any of the following prompts to journal on your relationship with incredible and unique *you*:

---

* June Jordan, "Where Is the Love?," Black Women Writers and Feminism panel, 1978, Carton 6:50, Barbara Christian papers, BANC MSS 2003/199 c, the Bancroft Library, University of California, Berkeley, accessed October 9, 2023, https://stories.lib.berkeley.edu/black-feminism/academy-1.

- What has your relationship been with self-love over the course of your life so far? If we are meant to master it, what stage of learning are you in?

- The opposite of self-love is self-loathing, which stems from our feelings of unworthiness. Has the feeling of unworthiness increased or decreased in your life? In what ways have you felt unworthy in your life?

- List some ways that you can increase the amount of self-love in your life.

- Do you think that life as a human is a gift? Do you live your life with gratitude to be alive or with dread? Why?

- List 10 things that you are grateful for in this life. If you are struggling, it can be as simple as the sun coming out today.

- Have you found your life purpose? If yes, reflect on the journey it took to get there—was there any correlation with cultivating more self-love in your life? If no, write about one small self-love step you can take right now that will allow you to set foot on the self-love soul path.

Chapter Exercise

Forgiveness is the fast track to self-love. Once we accept this truth, what do we do next? We can turn to the ancient Hawaiians for help with that. Hawaiians have a long-standing forgiveness practice called *Ho'oponopono,* which roughly translates into "to right a wrong." This practice is about restoring balance back to your heart.

A Hawaiian therapist, Dr. Ihaleakala Hew Len, used a form of Ho'oponopono while working with the mentally ill patients of a hospital for the criminally insane. As Joe Vitale describes it in his book *Zero Limits,* Dr. Hew Len went through each patient's file and repeated the mantra below as an experiment—and the results were incredible! The patients whom Dr. Hew Len held in mind as he spoke the mantra experienced healing and inner transformation, despite the fact that he was not working with them face to face. If anything illustrates that forgiveness is the pathway to freedom, this is it! Acceptance of self creates *infinite* possibilities of love for ourselves and others.

These are the steps of Ho'oponopono as described by Dr. Ihaleakala Hew Len:

- Close your eyes and think of someone you want to forgive (this can even be yourself!). Hold their image in your mind and their energy in your heart.

- Say the following mantra as many times as you feel is good, either out loud or in your head while continuing to visualize this person or yourself: "I'm sorry, please forgive me, thank you, I love you."

- Practice this forgiveness mantra daily and watch how your negative emotions begin to release and your heart shifts toward forgiveness, making way for more love in your life, both for yourself and others.*

---

*Joe Vitale and Ihaleakala Hew Len, Ph.D., *Zero Limits: The Secret Hawaiian System for Wealth, Health, Peace, and More* (Hoboken, NJ: Wiley, 2008).

CHAPTER 13

Pure Love

Everyone loves love. Everyone wants it. Everyone chases it. But what *is* love? If you were at a dinner party with 10 people and asked that question, you would receive 10 different answers. That's because love is the most mysterious force in the universe—and the truth is that we don't actually know that much about it. We know it's the best feeling in the world, we know we desire more of it in our lives, and we know we can look to poets and spiritual gurus to offer us glimpses into its nature, but we can't really come to a consensus on what it is.

Those of us who have undergone a near-death experience are lucky enough to be offered a backstage pass into the ultimate truth of both of those mysteries, and there is one nearly universal takeaway that all near-death experiencers share: Upon returning back to our human bodies, we understand that the meaning of life is to be and give love. Mastering love is the greatest lesson for us to learn as humans, and that's why relationships of all kinds are our most powerful teachers in life.

Near-death experiencers have this understanding because, from the lens of the spirit world, we learn that love is fundamentally *who we are*. As foremost near-death experience researcher Dr. Raymond Moody concludes from his decades of study of people who have died, visited the other side, and come back to life, "Whatever people were chasing before their NDE, afterward, they realize that what life is really all about is learning to love."* I think a more precise way to say this is that life is about *remembering* how to love—because where we came from before our birth into human existence and where we return afterward is built on the foundation of unconditional, pure love. On a core level, we already *know* love; it is our soul's essence. It's inherent inside every single person alive, though mostly misplaced due to the fears, insecurities, and limitations that make up the human condition. Our souls are pure love, but incarnating as a human means we develop blocks to love throughout our lives. Therefore, the mission of our lives is to do the spiritual work required to release our blocks to love.

One of the main reasons that we fail to reach a consensus on what love is exactly is that there are many variations of it, and they are not all created equal. If learning to love correctly is the goal, and we think again of our human lives as a school, there are levels of love, grades, so to speak, that we are meant to progress through. As humans, we are most familiar with the freshman kind of love: conditional love. But as we advance along our spiritual paths in life, we begin to understand the presence of a different type of love: pure love. And then as we simultaneously shed the conditional love and develop more of the pure love in our life in its place, we have the opportunity to understand firsthand the highest kind of love, the kind

---

*Raymond Moody, M.D., Ph.D, "Learning to Love," *Unity Magazine*, May/June 2022, https://www.unity.org/article/learning-love.

I've felt in all my forays in the afterlife: the pure love of Spirit. In this chapter, we will explore these variations of life's greatest mystery together and how, ultimately, to rise to the top of the class.

Conditional Love

Limits. Conditions. Tests. That is what humans do. And love is no exception. The "love" that most of us are familiar with as humans, though filled with moments of true beauty, can quickly become messy, chaotic, toxic, and even abusive. The reason for this is because we have a brain, because we think, and thinking creates distortions to the otherwise pure love that we are made of. In the spirit world, there are no distortions.

Here on earth, distortion is our default lens. That's why two people can have the exact same experience and understand it in entirely opposite ways. For example, our brains filter and perceive things according to our personalized views and life experiences. Thinking back to the little "heart-brain," recall that there is a growing view that the heart speaks to the brain more than the brain speaks to the heart. However, the heart does not have direct access to our mouths to communicate outwardly—the feelings and knowings of our heart *must* first filter through every cognitive area of our brain in order for us to speak them into existence. Everything we experience has to go from the heart up to the head to come out through the mouth. That's a long, winding journey. You can imagine that by the time we actually speak what is pure in our hearts, it becomes like the game of *Telephone*—the original message is lost. Distortions abound.

Enter conditional love. Because it deals directly with our human wounding, conditional love is a sensitive and complex topic. We all have wounds because we've all had childhoods—no one is immune! Even the most well-raised, well-adjusted children will grow up to be adults with core wounds to overcome during their lifetimes; it's simply an unavoidable part of the human-being contract. And, though we are all very capable of great acts of kindness, compassion, and love, much of our life is an attempt to soothe and protect these wounds first and foremost. In order to do that, we have a strong tendency to attach conditions to our affection toward other people—in other words, our love must be *earned*. Authentic, pure love doesn't need to be earned; it is given freely and often. In this way, the conditional love we are all so familiar with isn't really love at all, but fear masked as love.

Unless you were born a saint (and I haven't personally met anyone who falls under that category!), conditional love is your default way of expressing and receiving love in this world because, from the day you were born, that is what you have witnessed. Even if your parents loved *you* unconditionally, that probably didn't extend to all the other people in their lives. Conditional love is our baseline as humans with sizable egos. It is our way of self-preservation, a survival instinct. We think that by setting certain expectations on love it can protect us from disappointment and heartbreak, but the truth is that this approach ultimately does more harm than good, and we don't have to look further than the rapidly growing divorce rates to see proof of that. But it's not only romantic relationships that we apply our conditional love to—it's *every* relationship. The closest exception some of us have is our love for our children. Could you imagine if everyone loved everyone the way most of us love our children? What a wonderful world that would be!

As great as a worldwide love fest sounds, it's clearly easier said than done. Our brains have all kinds of justifications for keeping conditions on love in place, including our fears of rejection or abandonment, personal insecurities, feelings of unworthiness, desire for validation from others, and even cultural and societal expectations. By setting impossible expectations in our relationships, we are ultimately trying to manipulate the people in our lives to ensure that our needs are being met. But I'm sure you can see in your own life how well that works for long-term relationship happiness—it *doesn't*. Recognizing what conditional love is and what it feels like is the first step in inching further away from it.

So, how do you know if love is conditional? If you feel you have to earn it. If there are terms, rules, or restrictions surrounding your love, if the love is withheld during difficult times, if you feel extreme pain on the receiving end of someone's love, you are in conditional love's playing field. Conditional love is the kind of love that states, "I will love you *if* you behave exactly as I need you to." The key word is *if*. If you do X, I will love you, but if you don't do X, I will take my love away. Conditional love thrives on these kinds of control-based expectations. Most of us have heard the sentiment, "If you don't love me at my darkest, you don't deserve my light." Conditional love is love that rejects the darkness in another person—but the thing is, we *all* possess darkness. Every single one of us. And if we continue to reject the not-so-beautiful sides of the people we love, how can we ask them to love the whole mess of us? We can't, it isn't fair—and love like this will inevitably wither or else leave you in a world of misery. This is why the Golden Rule is a cornerstone in nearly every religion throughout history: until we learn to love our neighbor like we want to be loved, we will continue to feel disappointed in our relationships.

Again, easier said than done, but it helps to remember that learning to love each other the right way is a gradual process—the work of our lives, to be sure. Our job is to keep trying to learn to release the blocks to real, pure love. Ultimately, conditional love is rooted in the obsession to control our lives, which means that *surrender* is the key to releasing the limitations we place on love. Indeed, surrender is the fast track to pure love—the kind of love we are meant to reach for. Instead of attempting to use your will to manipulate every little thing that you feel afraid of, remember to trust that Yellow Brick Road that Spirit has neatly and precisely laid out for you instead of trying to build your own, and to accept that your will isn't the highest force to adhere to—Spirit's is.

Cleansing Our Distortions

Jayne Clark, a close friend and Energy Medicine Coach in Texas, reminds me, "We live on one earth, but we have 7.5 billion worlds." What does this mean in literal terms? Everyone is creating their own worlds through their own perceptions and beliefs on how they experience their lives. I often hear this comment: "Truth is truth, and love is love." However, I have learned that our different worlds change the shape of how we see things, baggage and all. We are all here on one earth plane; however, each of us carries inside of us our own personal truth and view of the world we are a part of. We all see things differently; therefore, our responses or views of the truth will never be alike. The one thing that is consistent in this journey is the actual fact of the matter: conditional love is not healthy or sustainable for long-term soul happiness, and it's not until we begin to shed those conditions we place on others and ourselves that we have the chance to *really* experience what true happiness and pure love feels like.

Just because conditional love is our default way of loving and it's hardwired into us doesn't mean that it can't be transcended. In fact, that is the goal. Again, the meaning of our lives is to learn (to remember) how to love—*the right way*. Distortions are inherent to this human journey, and they reliably make a mess of things, and our mission is to clean it all up as we go through our life, becoming purer in our love toward others and ourselves as we do so. I've personally gone through decades of cleaning up my unhealthy thinking, my damage, and my brokenness. My dark. It's challenging work, but it's the only work that brings us to the light. And it's vital for those seeking true spiritual fulfillment. Life creates the cracks in us; it breaks us down, that is unavoidable, and the pure love from which we came becomes distorted in the process. But it's our collective goal to cleanse those distortions throughout the course of our lives. As we do, we inch further and further away from conditional love and toward embracing pure love in its place. This is the big work, the big lesson of human existence.

When we understand that we are all one, we see that conditional love doesn't only hurt the other, it hurts us as well, and until we make the choice to walk away from it, we will be destined to circle in suffering. Luckily, we humans are built to overcome our shortcomings. And even though it is ubiquitous, conditional love is just that: a shortcoming that can be overcome. Learning to trade our default conditional love with pure love isn't easy, but it is our assignment as humans. And it is worth it because the more firmly we are centered in pure love, the greater the joy that surrounds our lives. The truth is that the one and only way that love can be true and last a lifetime is *unconditionally*.

Through self-reflection and developing our compassion muscle, we can learn to let go of the fears and insecurities driving our unrealistic expectations of others and embrace pure, unconditional love. In doing so, we can create a more empathetic and loving world, one in which everyone is accepted and valued for who they are and one where the veil between our humanness and our spiritual home begins to fade. As Ram Dass famously said, "We are all just walking each other home." And our home is pure love.

Aligning with Pure Love

The aim in life is to get as close to pure love as possible, yet we mustn't forget we are still humans! I would have a hard time believing someone who claimed to have mastered the art of basking in the high vibration of pure love *all the time*. It's important to give ourselves grace. As inherently flawed humans, there will always be the temptation to revert to fear-based behaviors—even monks lose their cool! But with a commitment to aligning with pure love and to learning to release our ego-based limits, we can become the purest love we possibly can here on earth. But 100 percent pure love? That belongs exclusively to the spiritual dimension.

In the world of spirit, there are no distortions. There, we don't have brains to interfere with the communication process; it's simply heart to heart, soul to soul. The angels that I encountered on my visit to the afterlife as a child embodied the purest love any of us could ever imagine—a love that is not bound by time, space, or human form but exists as a pure and unconditional force that connects all beings in the universe. I call this kind of love the pure love of Spirit. Though we will never fully become this kind of love until we return to the spirit world, the good news is that we can glimpse it right here, right now, more and more, through spiritual practices such as meditation, prayer, and other forms of spiritual contemplation. Tapping into the pure love of Spirit has endless benefits, such as fostering a more profound sense of connection in an isolating world and developing genuine meaning and purpose in our lives. Additionally, the pure love of Spirit is a love that provides comfort and solace in times of hardship and inspires us to live our lives with greater compassion. And, of course, aligning with spirit consciousness, this high vibration of love, helps make it easier to connect us to our loved ones who have passed on, spiritual guides and teachers, and the universe itself.

While pure love from Spirit may seem abstract or intangible, it is a *very* real and mighty force that can have a profound impact on one's life. Those who have been fortunate to experience pure love from the spirit world firsthand often describe it as a deeply transformative experience—something that can change your entire life overnight. This powerful love has cured terminal illnesses, healed deep-seated emotional wounds, restored hope, and brought forth a sense of purpose to those who have felt their lives are meaningless. By opening yourself up to the possibility of experiencing this type of love and, even better, practicing connecting to it, you can have a life rooted in peace and compassion.

For those who have had an NDE, the feeling of being enveloped in a warm and all-encompassing love like this is unforgettable. It's as if the boundaries between self and other, between life and death, have dissolved completely, and all that remains is an overwhelming sense of love and acceptance. All the barriers to love simply vanish—even if just for a moment. Whether you have visited the spirit world or have had spiritual visitations, know that the feelings of pure love and connection you experienced are *real*. They are not delusions. Trust in your experience. Embrace these incredible feelings, and allow them to guide you toward a life filled with pure love. By tapping into this love here in our human lives and allowing it to take the wheel, so to speak, we can experience greater joy—the greatest joy—in our lives. Pure love and pure love of Spirit are two powerful and transformative forces that can transform not only our relationships but also our entire lives. By cultivating a connection to these types of love, we can deepen our sense of connection to ourselves, others, and the universe, and ultimately, live a life that is grounded in the most powerful, most beautiful force in the universe.

❀ ❀ ❀

I want to end this chapter with the question with which we started: *What is love?* The glorious, eternal, pure love of Spirit that I felt on the other side while my four-almost-five-year-old body stood lifeless in a freezer—there are no words for it. We can try to define it, as I have tried in this book and as countless others have tried before me, but the fact of the matter is that we will not fully know until we *know.*

That being said, I can tell you with 100 percent accuracy that *pure love of Spirit is who we are.* It is our past, it is our future, and it is available for us to cultivate more and more in our present—we simply have to commit our days to reach relentlessly toward it. We must. It is our purpose, our inheritance. Like sunflowers that continuously turn throughout the course of the day to face the sun, let us keep our hearts fixed on pure love—until one day when we will *know*.

INTEGRATION MOMENT
Letting Love In

If you had to read aloud your personal history of love, how would that make you feel? Would you be embarrassed? Ashamed? Proud? Take some time to journal about your relationship to the various types of love—conditional love, pure love, and pure love of Spirit. By acknowledging where you have been, you can take the first steps toward where you want to go.

- Take a moment to reflect on a time when you felt a deep sense of love and connection with another person. What were the circumstances surrounding this experience? How did it make you feel? What can you learn from this experience about the transformative power of love?

- Consider the ways in which you currently cultivate and express love in your life. Are there any areas where you could deepen your practice? What steps can you take to connect more fully with the love that exists within you and around you?

- Reflect on any experience you have had with the spirit world, whether through dreams, near-death experiences, or other means. What did these experiences teach you about the nature of love and connection? How have they impacted your understanding of the world around you?

- Do you take moments in your day to express gratitude for the love that exists around you? Whether through prayer, meditation, or simply reflecting on the blessings in your life, allow yourself to fully immerse in the feelings of gratitude and love that arise. Trust that the love of the Universe is always available to you and that by cultivating a deeper sense of love and connection in your life, you can experience greater joy, fulfillment, and purpose.

Chapter Exercises

Are you ready to release the conditional love patterns in your life and start to tune in to the frequency of pure love? Use these exercises below to jump-start your journey toward unconditional, pure love:

- *Practice loving-kindness meditation:* This meditation involves cultivating feelings of love and compassion toward yourself, loved ones, and even difficult people in your environment. Start by sitting comfortably and focusing on your breath. Once comfortable, silently repeat the phrase, "May I be happy, may I be healthy, may I be safe, may I be at peace." While repeating these like a mantra, visualize yourself experiencing happiness, health, safety, and peace. Now think of someone in your life that you would like to send love and compassion. Visualize that person and silently repeat the phrase, "May you be happy, may you be healthy, may you be safe, may you be at peace." This practice helps you tap into the abundant well of pure love inside your heart.

- **Connect with nature:** Basking in nature is a powerful way to connect with Spirit and experience pure love firsthand. Take a walk in the forest, sit by your favorite body of water, or simply spend time in your backyard or local park. As you do so, allow yourself to fully immerse in the wonder around you. Observe how things organically work, whether it's the pull of ocean tides, the leaves changing, or the bees collectively working together. Being in nature reminds us of what is natural—and love is the most natural thing in the universe. Look around you; it is literally everywhere!

- **Practice an attitude of gratitude:** Cultivating more gratitude in your life is an automatic vibe raiser and helps deliver even more glory to your life. Take time each day to reflect on the things you are grateful for—even if it's simply the gift of being alive! This practice can help you tap into feelings of joy and contentment, and yes, love!

- **Engage in creative expression:** Creativity is an inherently spiritual practice. Art, music, poetry, and other forms of creative expression are powerful ways to connect with spirituality and invite more pure love into your world.

- **Reflect on what you have learned:** Consider how this book has made you more aware of yourself and those you choose to have around you. Take a moment to write some of the changes you want to implement to achieve peace and self-acceptance and cultivate love in your internal and external world. Return to all the Integration Moments and exercises you have written out in your journal anytime you feel confused about your journey and need to offer yourself understanding, love, and grace.

A Personal Message from Susan

Dear Soul Friends,

As you come to the end of *Infinite Life, Infinite Lessons*, I want you to know how grateful I am to have shared this time with you. This book was written for you to gain a deeper understanding of our fascinating universe and your personal soul connection to the spirit consciousness.

Thank you for your willingness and openness to explore and understand the deeper truths the spirit realm wants you to know. Your desire to delve deeper into your soul and its connection to Spirit took immense bravery; it may have changed how you view life and death!

I commend you for your courage to step into the world of spirit. I hope that *Infinite Life, Infinite Lessons* brought you healing, inspiration, and awareness of what awaits us all. May you gain *the knowing* as you explore this journey filled with peace, joy, and sorrow and walk life's winding road.

Writing about my journey with the spirit realm has served a higher purpose: passing down the lessons from my experiences to help *you* better navigate yours. I encourage you to embrace the signs and messages from the spirit world; the further you step into this realm, the higher you vibrate.

I invite you to remain open to Spirit's guidance to become the beacon of light you were *always* meant to be. Moving forward in your journey, use the lessons you learned while reading this book to motivate you and show you where to shine your light—*on you!*

As you continue on your journey, I want to offer a gentle reminder that you are never alone; the spirit world is always there to guide you on your personal path and to help you grow *through* the pain that this journey can bring and also help you reach your greatest gift, which is self-awareness and self-love.

The spirit world's love, support, and guidance are always there for you as you walk your intended life path. Trust in them and in the love they share with you. Use this guide to reach for your highest potential and know you are always loved and valued by the spirit consciousness that resides in a vibration next to us all.

While on your journey through life, I trust *Infinite Life, Infinite Lessons* will continue to motivate you and offer you the tools to fill the cracks that exist in your soul. I urge you never to stop expanding your consciousness, allowing a deeper awareness of why you are here and how you can grow on *your* beautifully chosen journey.

I encourage you to stay open to the spirit world and know they desire your *highest* good to resonate into the core of your soul. Guiding you to where your light can shine. May love, peace, and knowledge grow in you throughout your time here on earth.

Acceptance of hardships is the pathway to peace. My most genuine wish is that this book illuminates your soul with *hope*, as much as it did mine while writing it.

A special thank you to all of you and to my spirit team for every lesson I have been taught while walking *my* winding road to personal growth and self-love.

Remember that what we gain by reaching our destiny is not nearly as important as what we become by reaching toward it.

With love and gratitude,
Susan

Acknowledgments

While writing my book, *Infinite Life, Infinite Lessons,* I was truly blessed to have so many wonderful people in my life who have supported me, believed in me, and encouraged me. Thank you to everyone for bringing this book to fruition. Linda Konner, my wonderful literary agent, thank you for believing in this book and working tirelessly to find the right publisher to bring it to life. Thank you to my editors, Nicolette Salamanca Young, Lara Asher, and Anna Cooperberg, and the rest of the incredible publishing team at Hay House for supporting me and nurturing my book throughout this process.

I am so grateful for my talent agent, Meghan Amaral (M Media Corp). Thank you for your tireless commitment and hard work—the countless late nights and long days, reading and rereading every page to ensure it was as perfect as possible.

Thank you, Arizona Bell, for helping me find my words and communicate my ideas effectively. Your guidance, support, and creative talent were instrumental in shaping the *Infinite Life, Infinite Lessons* book proposal. Your talent precedes you.

I want to thank my friend, Sunny MacLaughlin, for reading every inch of this book more than once, crossing T's and dotting I's. Your sharp eye for detail, insightful feedback, and friendship have been invaluable.

Finally and most importantly, thank you to my husband, children, and grandchildren, whom I love beyond words. My love for you all has no bounds!

My husband, Dennis, your support has meant so much to me. You have been my rock, my sounding board. Without you, I would not have been able to achieve what I have accomplished. Your love and support have been the anchor throughout writing this book. I am grateful for all the nights you patiently waited for me while I locked myself away writing. Your belief in me has given me the strength to push through the tough times. After almost 40 years, you are still my everything. I love you more!

My amazing daughters, Jessie and Taylor, thank you for your love and support. Your encouragement has kept me going through thick and thin. I love you beyond words and am so proud to be your mom. Love you forever and always and to the moon and back.

To my son, Kevin. Thank you for being such a kind and loving man. I love you so very much! I always know you are in my corner, and I am grateful for you always.

My granddaughter Leila Grace, you are my precious girl! You are practically perfect in every way. You carry my heart. You inspire me every day to be better. I adore you; you make my life more than I could imagine. Nana loves you!

My grandsons Aiden and Kasen, I adore you both, and I am so proud of you. And to my grandson and grand-daughter Nolan and Alissah, thank you for making me a great-grandma to the newest member of our family, Evan Thomas. I love you all so much, and I am so grateful for every one of you.

My sister and friend, Peggy, I love that we hold each other's memories and that I have you on this planet to love and be loved by. Thank you for giving me my niece Sarah and great nephew Jacob. I love you all with all my heart.

I am so blessed to have you all as *my* family!

About the Author

Susan Grau is an internationally recognized intuitive and evidential medium, international speaker, and grief coach, whose talent *New York Times* best-selling author Riley J. Ford calls "unparalleled." As a celebrity reader with a benevolent, down-to-earth style, Susan has been featured in numerous magazines, podcasts, and documentaries, including Gwyneth Paltrow's *goop, ELLE* magazine, *The Hollywood Reporter,* M Media's *Susan Grau Hotel Series,* Elysium Media's *Beyond the Grave* documentary alongside Dr. Eben Alexander, and more. Having had a powerful childhood near-death experience, and since earning her Doctorate of Divinity in Mystical Arts with the father of near-death experience research, Dr. Raymond Moody, Susan is passionate about helping others, especially children, make sense of their afterlife experiences and leverage their newfound connection to the spirit world. Featured as one of James Van Praagh's exclusively preferred mediums, Susan is a gifted healer who is on a mission to help people heal the deep soul pain of grief by understanding the truth about the afterlife. Based in Southern California with her husband, Dennis, Susan is blessed with two daughters, a son, four grandchildren, a great-grandchild, two dogs, and a cat. Learn more at **susangrau.com**.

We hope you enjoyed this Hay House book. If you'd like to receive our online catalog featuring additional information on Hay House books and products, or if you'd like to find out more about the Hay Foundation, please contact:

Hay House LLC, P.O. Box 5100, Carlsbad, CA 92018-5100
(760) 431-7695 or (800) 654-5126
www.hayhouse.com® • www.hayfoundation.org

———

Published in Australia by:
Hay House Australia Publishing Pty Ltd
18/36 Ralph St., Alexandria NSW 2015
Phone: +61 (02) 9669 4299
www.hayhouse.com.au

Published in the United Kingdom by:
Hay House UK Ltd
The Sixth Floor, Watson House,
54 Baker Street, London W1U 7BU
Phone: +44 (0) 203 927 7290
www.hayhouse.co.uk

Published in India by:
Hay House Publishers (India) Pvt Ltd
Muskaan Complex, Plot No. 3,
B-2, Vasant Kunj, New Delhi 110 070
Phone: +91 11 41761620
www.hayhouse.co.in

———

Access New Knowledge.
Anytime. Anywhere.

Learn and evolve at your own pace
with the world's leading experts.

www.hayhouseU.com